PACIFIC ISLANDS
And South East Asia

0   500   1000   1500 kilometres

• PENRHYN
• RAKAHANGA
• MANIHIKI
NUKUHIVA
MARQUESAS IS

ORTHERN
OOK IS.

GHAUSEN •
SCILLY •
MOPIHAA •
RAIATEA
BORA BORA
HUAHINE
Papeete
MEHETIA
RAROIA
TUAMOTU
SOCIETY IS.
TAHITI
UTAKI
ERVEY
• MITIARO
MAUKE

AUSTRAL IS.
• RAIVAVAE

MANGAREWA

EASTER •

JTH   PACIFIC   OCEAN

GROWING UP IN POLYNESIA

GROWING UP IN POLYNESIA

Jane and James Ritchie

SYDNEY
GEORGE ALLEN & UNWIN
LONDON   BOSTON

First published in 1979 by
George Allen & Unwin Australia Pty Ltd
8 Napier Street, North Sydney NSW 2060
Distributed in New Zealand by
Book Reps (New Zealand) Ltd
48 Lake Road, Northcote, Auckland 9
New Zealand

This book is copyright under the Berne Convention.
All rights are reserved. Apart from any fair dealing for the purpose of
private study, research, criticism or review,
as permitted under the Copyright Act, 1956,
no part of this publication may be reproduced,
stored in a retrieval system, or transmitted,
in any form or by any means, electronic, electrical,
chemical, mechanical, optical, photocopying,
recording or otherwise, without the prior permission
of the copyright owner.
Enquiries should be addressed to the publishers.

© Jane and James Ritchie 1979

National Library of Australia
Cataloguing-in-Publication data:

Ritchie, Jane.
  Growing up in Polynesia.

  Index
  Bibliography
  ISBN 0 86861 201 4
  ISBN 0 86861 209 x Paperback

  1. Child development—Polynesia. I. Ritchie,
  James Ernest, 1929–, joint author. II. Title.

301.4314'0996

Library of Congress Catalog Card No: 79-51348

Set in 10.6 on 11.5 Times by Academy Press, Brisbane
Printed in Hong Kong

Contents

		Page
	Introduction	7
Chapter 1	Environments	15
Chapter 2	Communities	20
Chapter 3	Many Parents	27
Chapter 4	Being Born Into a Golden World	39
Chapter 5	Early Independence	49
Chapter 6	Children Together	60
Chapter 7	Achievement—With a Little Help From my Friends	72
Chapter 8	Gaining Status: Giving Respect	80
Chapter 9	Coming of Age	88
Chapter 10	Her World and His	95
Chapter 11	Early Education	106
Chapter 12	School and Community	121
Chapter 13	At Home and Abroad	136
Chapter 14	Human Development in a Pacific Perspective	146
	References	163
	Index	169

Introduction

In this book we will be talking about childhood in one tiny part of the world's population—the people who live in the islands of Polynesia and those whose traditional way of life derives from, or has been influenced by, Polynesian cultural style. We will try to identify the ways in which growing up in these islands differs from growing up in the other islands of the Pacific or any other place anywhere else in the world. At the same time the background to our thinking and to our writing is the general literature of child development—the stages and experiences through which children pass on their way to adulthood are necessarily and essentially human. So behind us we have the wide shelf of all that has been written about human development and before us we have the tiny shelf of books and articles about the Polynesian experience of childhood.

In the true anthropological sense there is no such thing as Polynesian culture. A Samoan is a Samoan, a Tongan a Tongan, a Maori a Maori and so on. Each island jealously defends its identity and we know that we run some risk in going beyond this level to generalise to the culture area. Historically, however, these islands are related; currently there are reasons for their peoples to look both ways—nationally and regionally; for the future there is no threat to individuality in seeing each island's tradition within the context of a wider sharing of culture patterns.

By Polynesia we mean the islands within that triangle of ocean classically defined by Hawaii to the north, New Zealand to the south and Easter Island to the east. Within this ocean setting the other major groups are, to the south the Tokelau Islands and the northern and southern Cook groups, to the east the Tuamotu and Marquesan archipelagoes and the group of islands around and including Tahiti, and in the centre the islands of Samoa and of Tonga. Other particular islands stand more or less isolated, Rotuma near to Fiji, Niue east of Tonga, Wallis and Futuna to the north. All these are within the triangle. Others, the so-called outliers, are set among cultures of a different history and association. They include Tikopia, Ontong Java, Kapingamarangi and Tuvalu (formerly the Ellice Islands).

Fiji stands on the boundary and is culturally marginal too. Its most ancient cultural roots are clearly Melanesian, as is shown by its language and mythology. But from the eighteenth century onwards it was considerably influenced by Tongan culture. Tongans came there to build canoes, and stayed for periods of two years or so whenever they came. They also came in conquest. Therefore the Polynesian overlay in Fijian life was considerable, particularly on the eastern side of Viti Levu and especially in the Lau group that spreads like a chain to the east, reaching almost to the Tongan islands themselves.

When we first began this book we excluded Fiji. There was not much information about childhood there anyway. But our students at the University of the South Pacific, both Polynesian and Fijian, insisted that Fiji be included and from their reports the similarities are so strong that it would be wrong to leave it out. Our own observations and discussions confirm this too, so, gathering such information as we can and aided by recent unpublished work, we have made the incorporation. We still feel just a little unsure about it. Not only do we lack the good field reports from a variety of Fijian settings that we would like to have, but we also lack any synthesis comparable to this one for Melanesia. Indeed such is the range of variation in Melanesian culture that this lack might never be overcome without considerable distortion of cultural realities. Maybe Fiji belongs in its own category.

We cannot write as though the world has never changed. And yet much of what we have to work on was written many years ago and by those who did not have direct experience of Polynesian childhood as Polynesians and who wrote as though what they saw was an unchanging pattern fixed in time. They often missed one essential message in Polynesian cultures, perhaps the most important of all, and so we come to state our first major generalisation about the cultures of Polynesia. These cultures changed, and are changing still, because the cultural traditions of Polynesia contain the implicit permission that a person or people can change, and change, and change, and still be the same. This is a profound paradox when stated in words, but a vital statement of reality when lived in the cultural context. The sea-going migratory histories of all Polynesian cultures carry stories of those who, coming to a new land, re-established the Polynesian way with vitality and integrity through adaptation. Change, as the essence of survival, has positive value. There are proverbs about it, tales and myths and songs. Yet the place names, the language, myths and values recur in island after island even though each is separate in space and in time.

This is our theme—persistence of pattern in a changing world. Even in those Polynesian settings like Hawaii or New Zealand where the people have, over the last six generations, encountered every possible cultural calamity save annihilation itself, the cultural tradition has survived. To do so there must have been powerful and pervasive ways in which young people were reared so that they came to act as carriers of the cultural tradition. More than this, they are today, as they have always been, right down to the individual level, creators within the tradition.

Florence Kluckhohn years ago made the simple but profound observation that every individual first becomes a creature of his or her culture, then a carrier and later a creator. All those around the young child and all the early experiences of childhood treat the child as the recipient of a whole set of cultural messages that no one can tell you about because they are simply 'the right way to treat young children'. Each in time becomes a carrier, a bearer, however highborn or humble, of these cultural messages and most will in time reproduce the unacknowledged memories of their own childhood as they rear their own children in what they consider to be the right way.

But since situations change, these cultural messages are always being reworked in everyone's experience, and so creative response is required of everyone. That sounds like an imposition, but in the sense in which we are speaking of creativity, and especially in the Polynesian view of what it comprises, being creative, far from requiring effort, is but a simple response to the ordinary challenges of everyday living—it is impossible not to be creative.

This book contributes to this process of successful adaption to change in Polynesia simply by making obvious what has been there all the time. It is not, therefore, a manual of how one might bring up children in order to make them Polynesian. Nobody needs such a manual. Its purpose is to bring together what others have said in a way which will, we hope, provide the people with yet another voyage of exploration on the great *Moana-nui-a-Kiwa*, the waters of the Pacific.

All we will do is gather the literature, a thin but rich harvest, and lay it before the people as one kind of offering to their continuing celebration of living the Polynesian life. It is a spare but choice feast that we prepare and season with our own experience of many of the places of which we write. As we invite the reader to enjoy it we also issue a challenge, particularly to the young who will become members of and leaders in their own cultures, to use it for the sustenance of their own folk. We have worked as best we could, given our resources. The resources of the people are always greater, for every Polynesian has both the right and the obligation to carry and to create within their own tradition. From within their own experiences and from the memories of their elders they may garnish and complement the ordinary food we have provided.

Naturally, since we have grown up in New Zealand, we will make a place in this book for the Polynesian people we know best, the New Zealand Maori. From their experience also has been derived the greater part of the small shelf of which we speak. Next in order of bulk in the literature come the islands of Hawaii; then the Northern Cook atoll of Pukapuka and then Samoa. There is a small literature on Tahiti to report and virtually single studies of Rotuma, Tonga, Niue, the Marquesas, the Tuamotus, Tikopia and the Tokelaus.

Much of this literature is now rather old but Polynesia had the good fortune to have as its first generation of ethnographers scholars of great stature: Ralph Linton, Margaret Mead, Raymond Firth, Ernest and Pearl Beaglehole and many more; what they have written remains of great value. Of course, how we were is not what we are but one cannot for that reason alone reject records so valuable. There often are no others. We are encouraged though by the way the pieces fit together and the way the major themes recur. These studies do not all report within a common framework. In any one study are great gaps which present and future generations of Polynesians may wish to fill. Yet there has been enough to satisfy us that we can write quite generally, since in doing so we are not really concerned with particular details of how the cultures differ.

Our first thought was to write one chapter for each culture. Some chapters would have been brief indeed and of some cultures we could have said nothing at all and by this omission perhaps caused offence. Had we chosen that approach we would also have emphasised the unique character of each and the differences between the cultures of Polynesia, and this would have been against our major intention.

So we have chosen to write of the major stages and the salient normal experiences of growing up anywhere in this island world and to draw on the cultures as examples. Thus the person from, say, Rotuma will meet his or her own island in many places along the way but will always see it placed within the common history, tradition and experience of the culture area as a whole.

Behind this aim we have two other motives, one very general and political and the other personal to ourselves.

The political motive is that while many occasions arise for the independent states of the Pacific to pull away from each other (and when they do so the media report such conflicts at length), there are few opportunities for the people of Polynesia to see themselves regionally, as a culture area, as cousins within a general historical fate. We hope this book can consolidate a common feeling of cultural kinship. This is especially needed in the multi-ethnic situations of places like Auckland or Honolulu or San Jose, San Francisco or Los Angeles, where each island community may be a small minority indeed but together they may be able to work such changes in residence, town planning, schooling, the administration of welfare that their common character requires.

The personal motive would not be obvious to almost anyone but us so we want to share it with our readers whoever they may be.

We are not ourselves Polynesian but have lived all our lives in New Zealand. One of us, Jane, was conceived in Pukapuka where her parents, Ernest and Pam Beaglehole, were engaged in the anthropological fieldwork which led to their ethnography of that island. She was born in Hawaii when they were writing *Some Modern Hawaiians*. The other of us, Jim, got his first insight into his future vocation from reading their best book, *Some Modern Maoris*. Both of us then began our own careers under their direction with our first research in the even more modern Maori community we called Rakau. For all of these reasons we dedicate this book to their memory. We wish we could place it in their hands as acknowledgment.

Later the ripples spread. Encouraged by all that work Howard and Gallimore and their group provided a new literature on Hawaii from which we have drawn extensively. When Robert Levy was going to Tahiti one of us cautiously helped launch his field work with advice that was designed to suggest ways of going about the job yet not prejudge the findings. Both of us have known Margaret

12 *Growing up in Polynesia*

Mead, first as teacher, later as friend, over nearly two decades, and she was a personal friend of the Beagleholes. We are drawing on all that experience as we bring this net to the shore.

What began fifty years ago as an attempt to describe the patterning of particular societies in Polynesia can now be drawn to at least a tentative conclusion, sweeping from the particular to the general, so that a new generation can go back to the particular again and begin a new cycle. We felt, therefore, that there was an inevitability about this book; its time had come. But also we know that it was needed.

Students labouring to prepare themselves as teachers have a right to see their own cultures reflected in some at least of what they read. They will, unless they are American, find little to satisfy this need in the usual textbooks of child development. Around and across the Pacific classes of young people and adults taking courses in continuing education may find more references in the general literature to the offspring of Jean Piaget than to their own background of cultural experience. For such groups we wanted to write an account that could be read alongside any standard text, confirming it in some respects and challenging it in others.

It is not only the received 'wisdom' of child development that we challenge here. As Margaret Mead did when she wrote about Ta'u in Manua (American Samoa) so long ago, we too take occasional glances over our shoulder at our own Western child-rearing, both as we and others have experienced it and as we and others have researched it. Our New Zealand students complained that when we did so in this book it seemed always that we were critical of the West and negative in our remarks. Perhaps so. If the reader wishes to hear what we have to say about our own, in more appreciative light, he or she might turn to our *Growing Up in New Zealand*. But we do not wish to seem to be using Polynesia either as a Utopian alternative or as a whip to beat the West. Westerners must follow their own fate and find their own solutions. But we are, in doing this, cautioning Polynesians against either free, enthusiastic, resigned or forced acceptance of Western models.

As we point out in detail later, the speed and pressure of change still bears strongly on Polynesian lifestyles. Whether at home or abroad peoples' lives are washed by forces that present the Western model of childhood, that style of family life and social relations as the only one or the best available, as necessary or inevitable.

If there is to be any conscious choice in such matters the nature of the alternatives need to be known. We will not argue for the preservation of Polynesian child rearing but merely for recognition of it. Its fate rests in hands other than our own.

Yet even as we wrote the book we reflected how far it was made possible and easy by the way in which, each summer, our own family changes gear and slips easily into a pattern of peer interdependence and play in the safe open landscape and seascape of the locality of our beach cottage. There for six clear weeks a year our children live with the freedom and responsibility that lies at the centre of Polynesian style. And as they disappeared into the environment doing what children will, so we went to our room to write and be grateful.

Often to become conscious of something leads not to a desire to change but just to the quiet sense of knowing that things are as they are, and that is how they should be.

Finally, we have a general concern for the future of us all. Western family style has reached the extremity of its shrinkage to smaller and smaller nuclear structures. Ways must be found to broaden the collective experience of children and lighten the load on the single parent who does most of the child rearing even within intact marriages. We all have to face the reality that nations everywhere are now multi-ethnic. Misunderstandings about parenting and the consequences of various styles have arisen and will arise. As social scientists our way of speaking to the future is to reveal what we think we know of the present.

At the head of each chapter we quote comments our students made on the text. They came from various parts of the Pacific and we were grateful for their help in the final writing of the book. It was, we like to think, rather Polynesian for us all to work together on the book in this way. We were also able to do the final editing at the University of the South Pacific in Suva, Fiji. So we also wish to thank the Vice-Chancellor and staff for their help and support, especially the folk in the Institute and the School of Education.

The book, however, is ours. We take full responsibility for it, errors, opinions and all. At least it was ours when we wrote it; now it has become everyone's.

Jane and James Ritchie
Te Whaanga
January 1979

CHAPTER *1*

Environments

> 'In the Samoas, life in Apia or Pago Pago can never again be thought of as communal in the sense of existing as a "whole community" like a village with interdependent responsibilities and social interactions. There has been some effort by our government to revive the authority of the matai in the traditional village of Apia, but things can never be the same again.'
>
> 'New changes have brought loose morals and a breaking away from the disciplined upbringing of children. New influences challenge the traditional values of education and child rearing and place greater emphasis on a money economy.'
>
> 'I was fortunate to have been exposed to several environmental conditions in my childhood. From an isolated village located in a river valley surrounded by mountains and forest where the main transport system was the river we moved to the sea coast. The food, climate, scenery and the people I came in contact with were all different. I learnt to get used to travelling long distances by sea, to get used to the strange sea creatures, to the waves and the rocking of the ship and to eating totally new and strange sea foods. I had to learn new skills like underwater fishing and the names of sea creatures. All of this was a totally new experience for me.'

Growing up happens somewhere—in an environment. Can anything sensible be said about the environments of Polynesia?

If you look at a map of the world the enormous oceanic distances of the Pacific immediately impress and it is easy to see why so often it has inspired lyrical thoughts of trackless wastes mapped only by the migrations of birds and creatures of the sea. But these days big planes make vast distances insignificant and it may be harder to get to the other end of one's own island than to another island culture hundreds of miles away.

To the people who live in these islands, the planes come, the supply boat arrives, the radio brings news. It is not so much the physical fact of vastness of scale that is impressive as the way, these days, people gaily hop from island to island. Where once only the bold or silly sailor made such contact now many people do (and unlike sailors they do not run the risk of getting lost or swamped along the way).

But it was not always like this and over centuries of isolation the various cultures of Polynesia developed quite striking differences. How far are these a matter of differing environments?

There is a whole school of thought which asserts that the way of life of a people is really determined by their environment. Such a view points to very obvious things—dry environments present particular problems for agriculture and thus provide fewer food resources than do wet ones. Coastal locations are a good source of food. Temperate climates require more effort to grow or gather sustenance, and clothing and shelter are more difficult and elaborate too. Continents make people conscious of political boundaries whereas on islands people may be more preoccupied with the internal structure of their societies. The environment will only carry a certain population and so when its limits to do so are reached people must resort either to migration, infanticide, abortion, warfare or other methods of reducing growth in numbers.

But there is more to culture than just a reaction to climate and geography, for culture is like human memory, a record of what people have done in the environment and found worth saving for the future instruction of those who follow them. When you reach towards the more profound expressions of culture in spiritual, religious and political terms, in the stories that are told and in the mythologies they reflect, the role of the physical environment is swallowed up in the record of the human uses of it. In the Maori case the word *whenua*, for example, brings to the minds of most people the idea of the earth, of the land, but to a pregnant woman the word would immediately arouse thoughts of the placenta which is nourishing her child and for which the word *whenua* is used in Maori, in Tongan and in other languages of Polynesia. When the child is born, the placental *whenua* is at times still buried in the original *whenua*, which is the body and flesh of *Papa-tu-a-nuku,* the original earth mother. It does not matter whether the land itself is dry or wet, hot or cold, sand or earth. Culture transcends environment. Polynesia, after all, covers high islands and atolls; it includes New Zealand, an island of almost continental proportions compared with almost any other Polynesian place. It stretches from tropical to temperate latitudes—yet always it is Polynesia and so we would expect to find the same link between the two *whenua* in deed (the burying of it in the ground) even if there is not the same word for it. The thought that links the two *whenua* cannot be reduced to any environmental determination. Nothing in the environment forced that association. It is a purely human cultural idea. That is what we mean by saying that culture transcends environment.

Of course the environment is important, always. And so is what people have done and are doing to it. There are now many places where one can no longer fish in the lagoon or where the population has outgrown the capacity of the physical basis that used to sustain and limit it. What then can be said about the environment within Polynesia in which children are now growing up? The most important considerations are in the contrasts that exist between the port and the hinterland in large islands or the headquarters and outer islands in the smaller groups. Leonard Mason has written about the growing differences in experiences between these two parts of the island world(74). Though he is speaking of Micronesia much the same sort of distinction can be made between village life and town life in places like Tahiti and the Samoas, or indeed almost anywhere in Polynesia.

In the urban headquarters ports the sense of whole community is no longer possible. They have grown too large to be thought of as though they were or ever can again be like villages. The authority of family heads and chiefs is strained, the role of formal education through schooling is more powerful and the differences and links between generations become stretched and strained. Individuals are drawn away from a belief in cultural authority, from the Polynesian background, perhaps even thinking of themselves as having a wider Pacific identity that replaces the community-based identity no longer available to them. Their diet changes from what they produce to what they can buy; the economy changes from working for the family or for the community to working for an employer for wages. Instead of living around an open village, children are confined in more restricted environments. There are new hazards like motor cars, electricity, broken glass and sharp tin cans. They may not even learn to swim. The entertainments of village sports and celebrations are replaced by movies, bars and hanging out on street corners. Old patterns of betrothal and marriage are overturned and the values of *Time* magazine begin to replace those of times past!

Yet important aspects of family relationships, such as the number of adult people to whom one may relate as though to a parent, or the importance of children of similar age (peers), or having another or alternative family, or the responsibility of older children to care for younger children, continue as part of the scene even in metropolitan Hawaii or New Zealand. There is no reason at all that these should not continue even though the Polynesian family seems to have been swallowed up in a great city like Auckland. But without a surrounding community it will be hard. For the future we need to be thinking and planning so that families in such cities will not suffer from individuation, isolation, boredom or worse.

The distinction between high islands and low islands is certainly very important in the island Pacific. High islands are of volcanic origin and show it, often dramatically, in their crested and crenellated ridges and high peaks. Often they rise thousands of metres above high water. Atolls are coral shelves rarely higher than a metre or two above the sea. In speaking with those who grew up on atolls we have been very impressed with the sense of home as a total place that is rather different from a high island. You can know and love every inch of it. An atoll's population has always necessarily been small and you know every person on it. The things you have around you and that you might play with or make things from are fewer. Crafts are limited to the materials available—tortoise shell, pandanus and coconut leaves, coconut shell, shells and seeds, and grasses. On high islands you have wood of many kinds, barks to manufacture *tapa*, and stone. All this in the past has made a difference. Perhaps it is disappearing now but there is still a simplicity about the natural atoll environment, especially on the outer islands.

A typhoon is a terrifying experience on any kind of atoll and hence, over centuries, the awareness of the dangers of natural hazards in atolls has been more deeply appreciated. If you have to lash yourself to a coconut tree while all the land there is becomes covered by rushing water and you are left without food, fresh water or the supplies to rebuild your home, then somehow, culturally, there must be some compensation for the contrast between that situation and the happier times of clear skies and warm days. Perhaps on atolls the closeness of social and family life may be a compensation. Perhaps, in traditional terms, atoll dwellers fashioned their gods against the possibility of climatic disasters while those on high islands had to take more account of human unpredictability. The cultural contrasts between the high and low islands have scarcely begun to be examined.

With the exception of New Zealand the existence of reef and

lagoon are an almost always present part of the Polynesian environment. They supply food, a safe place to swim and paddle one's own canoe, and protection, in some measure, from the violence of the ocean, though not on those atolls where the reef is the island, for there the exposure is great.

Historically it is possible that Polynesian culture grew and flowered on the high islands from which the atolls were peopled and probably repopulated from time to time(113). Atoll culture is ecologically very vulnerable. Yet larger low islands, like Tonga, for example, have been populated for a very long time and its people acknowledge no other origin.

Traditionally throughout Polynesia families were probably rather small until very recent times. For one thing, in pre-contact society, death, accident and some diseases held the population to certain limits and all Polynesian societies had techniques, which we will discuss later, of dealing with overpopulation. The survival of very large families is undoubtedly recent and the justifications which people make for them derive from the danger of extinction which followed the introduction of European diseases, disasters, warfare and economic exploitation. These effects were of appalling scope. On Ra'ivavae, for example, disease reduced the population from over three thousand in 1819 to less than one hundred in 1834(73).

Now there is virtually no part of Polynesia where the question of population limitation can be avoided. It may be hard to face up to the fact that, where once there were too few, there are now many Polynesians, too many in some places to be supported, or so many that the traditional life-style is threatened(47). The great need to have little children constantly around one probably arose from the fact that so many of them died. While there may be some distance to go yet in infant and child health, the great problem is no longer shall the children survive but how shall they be socialised to become carriers of the cultural tradition.

The physical changes which have been wrought in Polynesian islands have not only swung the people from traditional farming, hunting, fishing and gathering to more mechanised methods but have also begun, too often, destruction of the balance of reef and lagoon, of mangrove swamp and river, of forest catchment and flood plain. The switch from subsistence to cash economy is profound and increasing. But as with survival of children so too the persistence of the culture patterns in which they may be reared is not, in itself, imperilled. There will be changes—there always have been.

CHAPTER 2

Communities

'This is my fifth year at the University of the South Pacific and my seventh year in Suva. At times I felt that I have lost contact with my own people, that I no longer belong to the village but rather to the town. But this thought, I have found, is false. I still belong to the community I was born in. They are very willing to accept me when I go there during long holidays.'

'I have never had any feeling of alienation from my community. What they have, we share; my suffering is their suffering; my happiness and success is mine and theirs; my degree is a degree for myself and the community.'

'There is very little which I can see in my life that does not involve the whole community.'

'I know exactly to what community I belong, and consequently what mode of behaviour is expected of me.'

'As a child I was aware of the fact that I was always welcome in the homes of my "family". Their homes were mine as mine was theirs. None of these relations, including my parents, would ever question my being there for a meal or for a night's stay, or even longer.'

'The practice of collective action and sharing of responsibility in Polynesian society is not working in some areas here in New Zealand. I have known children of five or six years old to go "missing" for two or three days because mum has "thought the child was with aunty"! Rather than everyone caring, no one is caring.'

'I was taught to acknowledge the attention given to me by my older relatives by doing little tasks for them. A feeling of obligation was thus established between the older relatives and myself which I will have to fully acknowledge when I am working and earning.'

The word 'community' has become such an 'in' word in Western society (maybe because people have lost the real sense of its meaning) that we need to ask every time we hear it used just what it means. When a politician uses it it may mean as many as three million people (the New Zealand community for example) who never see one another face to face all at once and who have no means of acting as a whole except through the remote agency of government. A clergyman may use it to mean those people who see one another for just one hour on Sundays or some community of like-minded people otherwise quite remote each from the other who share an allegiance to a common ideology. But everywhere in Polynesia it has a local, specific and precise meaning. For example, in Samoa it is the *nu'u*, the village, usually of one extended family, *aiga*, whose separate households, *fua'i fale*, live in separate houses or *fale*. In Niue it is everyone, for the island is small. Though on Rotuma one half of the island is Methodist and the other half is Catholic, people are not confused as to what community they belong. The faces are familiar, the social map of status a reality. Even when people leave their own island to live in Honolulu, or Los Angeles or Auckland, and even if they do not seek their own kind in these locations, they know to what community they belong.

In the symbolism of a Maori proverb, 'by the seed that was scattered from Rangiatea I am never lost', one can always recover knowledge of the kinship that places one precisely within a real community, sometimes more than one but always one that is home. The proverb relates to the idea of *turangawaewae* (a place to stand), that through kinship one can claim enough land on which to stand up and speak with one's feet firmly on that which one possesses, as of right. On the one hand (or foot), *turangawaewae* is a very concrete fixed concept—it refers to particular and precise 'real' land. But on the other hand, since kinship may be traced through either mother or father and back through many marriages in many localities, it is a 'portable' and symbolic idea by which one can establish membership of community wherever one goes —even into an environment so alien and non-Polynesian as a city. As with so many things in Polynesian life, community is at one and the same time both powerfully real and, with equal power, symbolic. In the real sense, community is those with whom one lives, who are also one's kin with whom one shares common understandings of a moral and ethical nature that govern the ordinary course of life.

At the symbolic level, community is the hook on which one's identity hangs, the group from which one draws one's membership and for whose company one longs even when they are not around.

Community is more than just a circle of friends. Everyone has friends and misses them when they are not there, but not in the sense that a Polynesian needs his or her community to feel really whole. So important is this that the most powerful sanction that can be exercised by the group over the individual is rejection. This, we will see, derives its power from early experiences of childhood which create a diffuse sense of interdependency, *tatou tatou* (all of us together), rather than on single parents or exclusive relationships. In communities relationships are inclusive and people go to great lengths both to remain inside the boundaries of community definition and to hold or draw others in there too. The gossip, the circumspection, the subjection to authority, the pressures to conformity, the lack of privacy and personal space may often be oppressive but the deal is made, the bargain drawn; the negative and oppressive things about communal life balance out with the warmth, the support, the security.

How is this different from a small village in Massachussets or Queensland or Central Otago? The difference lies in the all encompassing nature of the community which reaches out and touches and indeed exerts authority over every aspect of life in each Polynesian setting. Through the rituals of oratory and the ceremony of meeting the community exercises political authority. The space between houses is the community playground, parade ground, political forum, a community place. All the community is involved in religious life, sometimes under parson or priest, but mostly through the offices of lay members which every church appoints. Those who work for wages may be called on to contribute to the general support of their wider family, to a particular financial need, perhaps a new house or a family wedding, and certainly for the building of a new church hall or community house. When the village is honoured by the visit of someone of distinction, or gathers to celebrate a life event such as a betrothal, marriage or death, the load is carried by all to see that the *mana* (prestige) of the person, place and occasion is properly acknowledged. There is nothing as total as this in Western societies any more, except perhaps in a few Utopian or religious communities.

Therefore, it is into this reality of community that one is born even though one may be thousands of miles away from its location. The community was there before one came and it will be there after one is gone. All the events of modernisation and social change have not altered this fact. The great challenges in the lives of Polynesian people arise from the reality and the necessity to work always in community terms. As populations have grown, and particularly as imported systems of political administration have brought new ways and other life styles, other ideas of other organisations to the islands, the importance of community life may seem to have been overshadowed, but this appearance is an illusion. There is a challenge in new Pacific nations to recognise it as such and to develop political systems and administrative practices which are directly related to the reality of community life and to work through it, not against it.

Community does not mean sweetness and light, universal harmony and every day a happy day. Because it contains many people, the life of a community is complicated and incorporates much diversity. It is *always* a problem to allow for the differences between people which *must* be respected. It can happen that when everyone expects someone else to take responsibility no one does. The life of the community must contain all the paradoxical opposites of human living in their Polynesian forms. For example, all Polynesian societies place great emphasis on status, but equally they emphasise democratic respect for each individual—the right of every person to speak, each in his or her own place and time. Women, though they seem to have lesser status, often have great power. Status itself contains the conflict of that which is inherited and that which is achieved, at any time for each person, both fixed and changing. The complexity of village politics in Samoa or Tonga or anywhere else arises as people try to hold to an ideal of consensus political action keeping all these things in mind.

When some years ago we started to list all the possible ways in which a small Maori community could find itself in conflict, between localities, lineages, religions, affiliations, immigrant and local born, historical insults and grievances and contemporary disagreements, we came to wonder how a community that contained so much conflict could be a community at all(92). But working there, we slowly came to realise that all these sources of disagreement were expressing what that community was really all about. The people could voice such differences, usually quite openly and often quite vehemently, just because they were a community. This means that the value placed on community was wider and stronger than any other value and woe betide anyone who, through misguided goodwill, took upon themselves the task of resolving conflicts prematurely. The community that fights together stays together!

So here is another paradox. At one time the whole community will rally together to prepare a feast, all thoughts of conflict forgotten, and the very next day, in discussing the event, all the divisions will appear as though yesterday's harmony had never occurred(92).

In this all-encompassing sense of community, what happens to privacy? Anywhere in Polynesia you find people place value upon it, increased because it is so rare. Personal privacy, even within the household, is something that must be protected and often worked for and if it cannot be attained, then given up. Coupled with this is the sense of modesty and shyness about private and particularly bodily functions. The adoption of the long dress style for females, for the introduction of which the missionaries are usually blamed, was made easy by this attitude, and not forcibly imposed as some think. Proper and becoming female behaviour always and everywhere implied a quiet reticence that was traditional long before the white skins arrived. Even accidental genital display was and is quite abhorrent; when you swim or sit you tuck your *lavalava* between your legs lest you unwittingly give offence, yet within the *fale* a simple *tapa* curtain has to be enough to make public space private.

For the young person growing up, and particularly for the adolescent, the lack of privacy and the constant surveillance within the community may often seem oppressive. And whereas there was once no chance to get away because there was nowhere to go, it is now all too easy to leave the community at will, or all too necessary, in some cases, to go elsewhere for work or education. In a modern world of free choice beyond the community's authority, new ways of being Polynesian must evolve which permit people to re-enter the community or to maintain the warmth of their membership even though they are far away. Many do this by increasing the intensity of their experience when they return, even if only for short visits during the annual vacation. But many do not; there are so many difficulties—the cost of travel, the alienated feeling that so much has happened while one has been away, the shifts in family status, the obligations that should have been met and now perhaps can never be fulfilled. Some who return may feel great pain however warm and receptive their welcome; sometimes this is not lessened by the reaction of the community which may raise all the anxieties of rejection in the heart and mind of the homecoming exile. Rather than suffer this the exile may stay away, the tension growing greater not less as time passes. But our Pacific students tell us that though after many years away many felt reluctant to return, when they did their community made them welcome. Though they themselves felt alienated and distant from their home villages, the community was ever ready once again to receive them back as though they had never been away. There is a challenge to both those who go and those who remain to develop from that mixture of longing and loving which Maoris call *aroha* new patterns for the future that will reduce conflicts of this kind. In the Western world that so values progress and advancement it may well be true that having left home you really can never wholly return. Absence may close doors that can never be reopened; you may so grow away from your roots that from shame or pride they cease to mean very much. That is rarely, if ever, true in Polynesia. Whereas in the European world you grow up in a family, in the Polynesian world you grow up in a community, real or symbolic, present or distant. It is not always easy, but it is Polynesian.

When a Samoan moves from village to Apia or further to Honolulu or San Mateo, it may seem that community is lost and gone forever. That can happen and within one generation those persons or that family become psychological as well as physical migrants into the new setting and may feel that they never want to return and are unable to do so. But simply to recall in the right setting the family name and ancestry is enough for social placing to occur back into a community setting. And increasingly in those urban places a new kind of community is developing, functionally very different from the rural village yet re-expressing basic cultural values of reciprocity, sharing, consensual politics, communal festivals and worship, respect for authority and status and so on.

Finally, let us ask again what is Polynesian about Polynesian communities. They have closely related languages, between which, once consonant shifts are allowed for, there is some intelligibility and certainly common linguistic structure and basic vocabulary (16, 76). They have a common cosmology and mythology behind their traditions. In all, the world emerged from *Kore*, the formless original night. They all personify the sky as father, whether they term him *Rangi* or *Atea* or *Rangiatea*, and derive their sustenance from *Papa* the earth mother. Four common gods (or their dialectal equivalents) derive from four attributes of existence: *Tane* for humanity, *Tangaroa* for the ocean as highway and as sustenance, *Tu* for conflict, warefare and death and *Rongo* for the vital and ever present peaceful world of agriculture. Some give precedence to one of them, others to another. They all contain the equal endorsement of two strong cultural themes, the one which enjoins conservatism, care and caution and the other innovation, creativity and change. They all place great stress on status and status rivalry and the enjoyment of the challenge and response which derives from it as expressed in oratory. They all emphasise genealogy, time depth and the place of the individual in cultural continuity. All of this was summed up by Margaret Mead when she spoke of the robustness and strength of the survival of Polynesian cultures which are able to retrace, in her phrase, 'their long voyages into the present'.

Every Polynesian can inherit this tradition in its own island form, expressed in his or her own village background or the background of the parents' or grandparents' place of origin. As Mead said, the contemporary inhabitants of Pitcairn, who inherited a pitifully small sample of Tahitian culture, have been able to construct for themselves their own particular version of the Polynesian way and it is interesting that, although the alternatives were to be English or Tahitian, they became Polynesian Pitcairners(76). It was the Polynesian identity which survived. Perhaps this is because, at the core of the cultural continuity lies the particular relationship between women, children, and the community that surrounds them. In the last analysis the person who instructs the young is the final arbiter of what enters or leaves the succession of cultural continuity over generations. But even before that, the most basic level of all, of experiences before one had language to express them, of feelings about oneself, the outside world, other people, the first and last inescapable patterns of cultural identity, was laid by whatever it was that everyone around shared. To search for that, and to find it, to know it, is to appreciate who one is and who one's children shall become.

CHAPTER *3*

Many Parents

'As far as my childhood was concerned, family meant the nuclear and extended families together. When I was a child, I never saw my family as only father, mother, brothers and sisters. My childhood experiences involved interactions with grandmothers (both grandfathers were dead before I was born), aunts, uncles, cousins, great uncles and great aunts and so on. These relatives gave me as much attention as my own parents gave me.'

'Being the eldest of three children, I was a special child to both grandmothers and aunties. My parents rarely gave me the stick or told me off in the presence of these doting people. I used to feel proud of those moments when either my grannies or my aunties told my parents off for being cruel to me.'

'A Polynesian child belongs to everybody and vice versa, whether he is an adopted child or not. Aunts and uncles have equal rights in punishing the child when he does something wrong.'

'It was rare for the natural parents to be pointed out as the cause of a child's bad behaviour. The whole (extended) family was shamed whenever a child was considered ill-mannered or badly behaved.'

'A woman may be ashamed for her infertility as a result of casual teasings from her sisters-in-law. This is quite common in my society (Fiji). Comments like "cassava-waster" are made, meaning that the barren woman was not making good use of the food provided by her husband by giving the latter a child. These comments are even uttered to women who give birth only to baby girls, without a son to carry on the line.'

'Caring for a child is a cooperative effort of the relatives or of the community at large. I have often heard older folks telling young parents to give some food to a crying child even though the child is suffering from over-eating.'

'I know of some adoptees who run away to their real parents when they get old enough to know. Others don't seem to care—they've happily taken on two or three homes with the full knowledge of who their real parents are and who their adoptive parents are.'

'My parents, like others in the village, expected my relatives to have parental responsibilities over me. If they failed to do so, they were considered "bad" relatives.'

If communities are the context within which children grow, the family is the lattice of correction and support that gives direction to that growth. The analogy is precise for in Western families the single-mindedness of parental control and direction is like a straight stake holding the child's development correctly. In Polynesia the influence comes from many, all of whom carry the same messages about what is right or good or correct.

In the Western family even where there are two parents the allocation of roles to men and women make children and childhood women's responsibility so children are, for the most part, reared by virtually one parent only, mother, with less certainty or constancy about the role of the other, father. In Polynesia a person has *many* parents most of whom are continuously available.

Multiple parenting arises out of kinship, community and close living residence patterns. Its effects are early, deep and all pervasive. When you have many parents the social world of affection and attachment spreads wide, the admonishing voices that reprimand are not personal but collective, the hands that reach out to cuff or slap or check are neither impersonal nor personal but somehow both.

As Margaret Mead says, 'a child of three can wander safely and come to no harm, can be sure of finding food and drink, a sheet to wrap herself up for a nap, a kind hand to dry casual tears and bind up her wounds'(75, p. 40).

Every Polynesian knows who his or her 'real' mother or father may be, but beyond them lie all those who may act parentally —and that is a wide network reaching out into kinship and community.

Throughout Polynesia a similar type of kinship system is found but Western anthropologists have had considerable difficulty in saying just what the word 'family' means. The most obvious reason for this is that there is no Polynesian word for family and the various equivalents, *whanau* in Maori, *aiga* in Samoa (where *fanau* means children), *wanau* in Pukapuka, *feti'i* in Tahiti, *kainga* in Tonga are, in a defining sense, rather abstract. Let us explain what we mean.

When a European says 'my family', he or she means the nuclear set which may be extended backwards to the parents whom the person grew up with (anthropologists call this the family of orientation), or downwards, to include one's descendants or descendants of descendants (the family of procreation). While this is a small group it has three primary defining criteria: it is a group of clear, biological descent, it is residential in household terms (for the most part), and it is an emotionally closely bonded group of people.

Within Polynesian experience the biological descent quality of the family needs not be emphasised because it is taken for granted and the prime criterion of the family is social. Where everyone is related some other demarcation of family is necessary. Traditionally, the social mechanisms that bound a family together centered around a group of people who were an economic unit —they worked together for mutual support. It was also an allegiance group in which one knew one's place, genealogically, in terms of status and identity. Nowadays that is not always the case and inevitably it is the occupants of a household, or those who cook, eat and sleep together, that defines the primary social group.

Nowadays European words concerning relationship have crept into Polynesian languages as, for example, where the terms *matuatane*, *tamai* or *tama*—all traditional words for father—have been replaced by the English borrowed word *papa*. Burrows, however, says that the true Polynesian use of the word *papa* referred to mother (as in Tongareva)(20). To anyone familiar with basic and common Polynesian mythology the reason for this is obvious, since *papa* is derived from the name of the mythic earth mother, *Papa-tu-a-nuku* (as opposed to *Rangi*, the personification of the sky who is the primal father). In most of Polynesia the term that comes closest in meaning to mother is one or another of the dialectal forms of *whaea*, which in Maori usage refers to the biological or adoptive mother and the sisters of the father or mother. A Maori person might well say of an appropriate woman, 'she is really my *whaea*'; this means that the person spoken of acts towards the speaker as if she were the mother. In other words, there is no functional distinction between the father's sisters, mother's sisters or mother. They all come into the classification or category *whaea*. The anthropological textbooks use the term 'classificatory kin' to refer to categories of people who, though not the biological relative, act in the same capacity. But the term is not very useful since all kinship terms are classificatory. The native speaker is not the least bit confused about using the same word for his or her biological mother or father as for their collateral kin referred to by the same classificatory name. They act in the same general way, as parents, but some are closer than others. So when a Western anthropologist such as Metge starts to hunt for the functional meaning of the Maori transliteration *whamere* (family) she really has a difficult time(77). She is trying to find a modern meaning for something that has no traditional equivalent. One respects her effort and the complexity of the problem, especially since the people she was studying were busily engaged in building a new form of urban culture from their past rural base. Things, as we said, keep on changing all the time.

Just as one can learn much about a culture from concepts that are peculiar to it, so too one can gain insights from the absence of an idea. There is no real Polynesian equivalent of the Western concept 'family'; all terms that seem like it refer to extensions that include many people beyond the nuclear family unit. Around the Western concept of family a great part of the literature of Western child development and sociology has been written and to attempt to apply all that theory to cultures that lack the concept on which it turns is simply unprofitable at best and ethnocentric or even prejudiced at worst.

In many Polynesian languages the word *whanau* occurs in some form or another and in a rather sloppy way, or perhaps in desperation searching for something equivalent to the family concept, Westerners have often regarded it as broadly equivalent to their word. This it is not. The term (or its dialectal equivalents) refers to the blood bond that exists between members of a tribe and the emotional allegiance which that implies. When a Polynesian uses such a word he or she casts a very wide net. We might say that *whanau* derives its emotional impact from the extent of its inclusiveness whereas the Western concept family gains emotional intensity because the 'we' it identifies excludes all the rest. There is a whole cultural world of difference here.

Actually, if you listen very closely to speech-making, the various terms for a collectivity of kinsfolk are on a gradient not of political hierarchy but of emotional familiarity. Addressing a group for the first time, or at psychological distance, a Maori orator might refer to his hosts as *iwi*, later or at lesser distance as *hapu* and when he feels really close in psychologically, as *whanau*. One might even use the term *whanau* for a very mixed bunch from different tribes to try to overcome the looseness of relationship or the tension of strangerhood. Only in a loose way is *whanau* the equivalent of family.

In fact, the Western family concept, historically and legally, has a great deal to do with Western concepts of property and inheritance. The boundaries of the family were drawn tightly and exclusively lest inheritance be watered down. Polynesian societies were simply not organised that way because land and property were not exclusively owned. The external boundaries of a society were territorially defined but within it the preoccupations were with social relationships, social placement, status.

So that when one looks at such things as kinship terminology one sees contrasting pairs of terms that signify contrasting kinds of relationships between pairs of individuals within the tribal group that are of importance in expressing obligations and rights. The organisation of these pairs is based on two biological facts, seniority and gender. The terminologies, furthermore, are all relative to the speaker. This is best explained by an example from the New Zealand Maori kinship terminology system. The term *tupuna* or its various dialectic equivalents always refers to a person two generations older than the speaker while the corresponding contrast term, *mokopuna*, always refers to a person two generations younger. Thus, it is often inaccurate to translate *tupuna* as old person or ancestor (though it may mean this in certain circumstances or contexts); it simply refers to a generational difference and you have to know who the speaker who is using the term is in order to be more precise. Similarly, though *mokopuna* is colloquially equivalent to grandchild, it really refers to a much wider set of youngsters. It is simply impossible to describe Polynesian kinship in general abstract terms. It always comes back to the individual who is describing his or her own kin.

Thus, when a person uses the term *matua* he or she is referring to all those people who have acted parentally. The contrasting terms are *tama* and *hine*, all those male and female children to whom he or she acts parentally. Such *tama* or *hine* need not be direct biological offspring nor even close kin. The term specifies a way of relating, a set of expectations that certain obligations apply, that certain respect shall be given, certain duties performed and acknowledged. The terms always indicate a special quality of relationship which has nothing directly to do with the degree of biological kinship. Thus a *tupuna* has a special affection for and affiliation with a *mokopuna*—the polarity implies special care, regard and affection. The pair *matua*, *tama* implies respect upwards and a disciplinary responsibility downwards. Similarly there are terms by which a person refers to an older brother or sister and a younger brother or sister.

Always to an older relative one gives respect, to a younger relative one gives care, however close, however distant. There are also widespread terms that distinguish mother's brother from father and father's sister from mother. There is really no exact equivalent of the Western terms aunt and uncle though Polynesians use these terms often and loosely; mother's brother is referred to usually by a different term from father's brother. In a modern context the term cousin has come to mean anybody who is a relative of the same age or younger than the speaker. Similarly uncle and aunt have come to mean any relative older than the speaker who is not specifically *matua* or *tupuna*. These days, one does not even have to be able to specify the kinship (there may not even be any and the terms uncle and aunt will still be used to express a relationship that is only fictionally kinship).

In traditional times there were some special features of Polynesian kin relationship. Brother–sister avoidance was clearly found in Samoa, Tonga, the Tokelaus, Futuna, Uvaea and Tongareva and in other places, though less clear, is present as a matter of respect and distance. In Pukapuka avoidance was prescribed between cousins of opposite sex, but not between brother and sister(7). The degree of avoidance varied from a simple modest reticence in one another's presence in some cultures to the extreme in Tongareva where a sister must avoid the wind that has passed over her brother's body. Margaret Mead describes the Samoan practices thus:

> Relatives of the opposite sex have a most rigid code of etiquette prescribed for all their contacts with each other. After they have reached years of discretion—nine or ten years of age in this case—they may not touch each other, sit close together, eat together, address each other familiarly, or mention any salacious matter in each other's presence. They may not remain in any house, except their own, together unless half the village is gathered there. They may not walk together, use each other's possessions, dance on the same floor, or take part in any of the small group activities. This strict avoidance applies to all individuals of the opposite sex within five years above or below one's own age with whom one was reared or to whom one acknowledges relationship by blood or marriage'(75, pp. 41–42).

The practice reflects social prohibition on incest. Probably it also has something to do with the widespread prescription that brothers were responsible for their sisters' virtue—a practice which must have given problems to both parties. This is simply another part of the way in which Polynesian societies distributed the care and responsibility that Westerners allocate rather more exclusively to parents. It is picked up again in the emphasis, often a ceremonial bond, between a male child and his sister's son, or his mother's brother. The variations in this can become very complicated.

In Tonga the sister of one's father has very high status and a special role. Her authority supersedes that of both the mother and the father and must be acknowledged whenever she is present (and often when she is not).

Whatever the traditional functions of all these kinship specifications may have been, and however much cultural change may have reduced or changed the emphasis on them, it remains true that Polynesians, when they meet another person from their own culture relate to that person in terms of kinship distance, gender, higher or lower generation and senior or junior status. When another person has been fixed in kinship space in this way, each individual, having located the other, knows what is expected of him or her. Westerners rarely extend parental privilege and obligations and duties to anyone else but the biological mother and father. Polynesians will always spread them and share them.

The balance between social and biological factors in Polynesian kinship can be seen particularly when one considers adoption. In the Western family adoption is rather rare and is generally of individuals who are not biological kin. It is done in rather private, almost secret ways, and often not admitted; names are not revealed, largely because the adoptee was born in circumstances regarded as shameful (illegitimacy) and because the adoptors also may feel some shame at their own lack of fertility. In Polynesian villages illegitimacy cannot be concealed and so is of relatively little importance. Infertility may be considered sad, or rather a joke that someone might be teased about, but generally it is not shameful and must be compensated for by other kinsfolk providing the children that the couple cannot themselves produce.

In the West, most adoptions are by strangers of strangers, whereas in Polynesia adoption is a transaction between close relatives. Carroll says the adoptor is often related to one of the natural parents of his or her adopted child as a full or classificatory sibling or parent(21). Whereas Western children are generally put out to some agency to arrange the adoption, it is rare for Polynesian parents to do so. Western adoption is characterised by formal legal procedures but this is not so in Polynesia (or at least was not so till very recently); adoption was a family and community matter. In Polynesia children are often adopted by a single individual but in the West almost always by couples. Most Western adoptors are childless while adoptors in Polynesia frequently have children of their own. Moreover adoption is much more frequent than in Western countries and the adoptors seem much less choosy about the physical attributes of the child they get; indeed a child may be adopted even before it is born. Prospective adoptors in Polynesia are rarely denied the privilege of adoption by economic circumstance or health or personality characteristics. They normally get no kudos for adopting another's child while natural parents who give up their children in adoption normally are not stigmatised; on the contrary, they are usually considered generous. The natural parents of Western children who have been adopted are unable or unwilling to assume parental responsibility. In Polynesia the natural parents of adopted children are usually ready, willing and able to keep their children but are culturally required to yield the child to the claim of another.

In Polynesia there are no intermediaries or adoption agencies, no vetting, scrutiny or references required, no bureaucratic approvals; if the adoptive parent proves unsatisfactory or incapable, other parenting persons are around and they or the biological parents may simply take the child back or take it over. The West regards adoption as altruistic; Polynesians just regard it as normal. The cultural emphasis is on the needs of those who become the parents, rather than on the needs of the child or the biological parent or parents of the child. In the West, adoptive parents who express a strong personal motive for adoption, for example at the death of their young child, may be regarded with suspicion by adoption agencies, whereas in Polynesia such needs are regarded as important and so are recognised and met. The idea that children might be adopted by total strangers is regarded with horror in Polynesian cultures, for you have lost a member of the kinship and therefore a potential member of the village workforce—and part of your blood. One need frequently recognised is that of *tupuna* who want a *mokopuna* to comfort them in their otherwise childless old age. The natural parents tend to resume parental authority should the adoptive parents die.

This traditional situation is, however, breaking down in the city where shameful pregnancies do occur (shameful because they are outside the kinship, tribal or even ethnic group), where economic circumstances may make solo parenting highly stressful and where, because more children survive now, a child surplus may be occurring. The Polynesian adoption practices were clearly a way of ensuring the survival of the child as well as of distributing its 'ownership'. In many large Polynesian cities, mixed race children will be dealt with by the formal machinery of adoption agencies rather than through cultural practice. Once the traditional village ceases to be the economic unit, then the whole pattern of social as well as kinship relationships begins to change and the life-style of potential adoptors is so different that adoption is no longer automatic. A child's mother may well be in full time employment and not able to undertake the care of a young baby born out of marriage as she would have done in a rural location. A mixed race child is not always regarded as acceptable, even though all Polynesian populations are now genetically very mixed. The biostatisticians tell us that there are now white or other foreign genes in every Polynesian. Perhaps it is this fact itself that lies behind the frequent but rather racist rejection of mixed race children!

Given the universality and the ubiquity of adoption in Polynesia it is perhaps curious that almost everywhere in Polynesia people make a distinction between fostering and adoption and that this distinction is essentially the same as in the West. In adoption the natural parents give up final and legal authority over the child; in fostering they do not. No doubt this relates to the central importance of genealogy but if this were that important, why is adoption considered at all? Whereas a fostered child keeps his or her original genealogy, an adopted child may claim both lineages, that of the couple he or she was born to and that of those who became the primary caretakers.

On the face of things, Polynesian cultural practices concerning adoption seem in human terms to be affirmative, positive and sensible, since they are supposed to provide distributed parenting and security for all concerned. An adopted child is presumed to have the rights and status of a natural child—whether a person is one or the other is not supposed to make any difference. We are not so sure of this, for we have spoken to many adopted Polynesians who felt abandoned by their natural parents, particularly if the adoption took place, as sometimes happens, in childhood rather than infancy and especially if the adoptive parents were very old when they took the child and died before the full span of parenting to adulthood was complete. The emotional significance to the individual of being an adoptee, while it may well be less traumatic because the fact of adoption has been known to them all their lives, may still be stressful especially as social change removes the real securities of village, family and group within which the Polynesian adoption system functioned. Indeed the dislocation caused by death of aged adoptive parents may be deeply resented.

As social change continues the Polynesian practices of adoption will necessarily undergo change and this may be considerable, especially where property is being dealt with in a framework of Western economic values. For example, the advent of family benefit payments in New Zealand forced Maori customary adoptions towards the Pakeha pattern of court approved legal adoptions since the state had to know to whom to pay the benefit. Undoubtedly this has introduced some rigidities into what was otherwise a flexible pattern, increased bureaucratic interference in family patterns and required legal representation. Furthermore, suddenly Pakehas became aware that Maori practices were different and interpreted the flexibility as neglect and evidence of, and condonement of, immorality. Thus, there is in adoption a hidden set of value judgments and an emotional charge that may have affected race relations and been affected by them also. Misunderstandings concerning adoptive practices and attitudes may become the basis of some inter-ethnic ill feeling.

The principle of collective action, the central foundation of the Polynesian way of life, is expressed in these kinship matters, including adoption. Polynesians need to be aware of this all the time so that they can evaluate where they are moving in the modern world. It will not be enough for Polynesian communities and parents to simply assume that their way of life can continue unchanged in these matters. They are surrounded by political, legal and educational machinery, including the literature of child development and sociology, which is based on a totally different set of premises. What Polynesians tend to accept as the necessary realities of modern living and a technological way of life are not that at all, but merely one set of options. Critics of the nuclear family style have not been slow to point out that the Western family derives from the particular nature of one set of historical forces. Not so long ago women and children were implicitly regarded as part of the possessions of the male, on whose shoulders rested full political, moral, economic and legal responsibility. His control was virtually absolute and bolstered by both Church and State. The Polynesian system balanced that sort of autocracy with the wider network of democratic responsibility and balanced the sex roles far more equally.

As the Western family is the breeding ground for Western culture, so the Polynesian kingroup is the surrounding context within which one becomes Polynesian.

In many places and in many ways we have tried to explain these sorts of difference to groups of people such as social workers, policemen, educators, parents' groups, students. But it is perhaps more important that these changes be appreciated by young Polynesians, for to lose these patterns of relationships and the terms that express them is to lose part of the essence of Polynesia. But, let us be clear. There have been studies enough of the anthropology of Polynesian kinship for its basic system to be known and to be understood as far as it can be and needs be. It is not research that is needed now but awareness. The Polynesian family system will not survive unless young Polynesians are given the opportunity to know and appreciate how it is different and why that difference should be expressed in every aspect of the modern life of Polynesian people. What kind of education system is it that provides children with the chance to learn the genealogy of British royalty and never provides them with their own?

Finally let us return to the theme with which we opened this chapter. We have argued that community and family are identical in the village, island or rural situation. We would argue that they can continue to be something like that in the metropolitan or urban setting. But to achieve this requires conscious planning. Why should anyone bother about this?

When one's cultural background to growing up includes many adults sharing the roles and responsibilities of being a parent, the strain on any one person is reduced(14, 78). When that cultural background is abandoned or a family deprived of it or the social networks that derive from it are lost, there is not always distress or the shock of culture loss. Not always, but certainly very, very often.

So modern Polynesian parents may not have that other adult around to take care of the children while they go off to a meeting or celebration, a movie or the pub. Children may be left alone or left in the car. The village was a natural crèche—where is the city equivalent of that? So when modern children feel aggrieved with their parents, have a 'row' or are punished more harshly than they feel is right, where are the other 'parents' to whom they can turn for refuge? Old Polynesia had no runaways and if children took over an unused *fale* or *bure* as a sleeping house all their many parents knew, knew why and understood. Now children may be left confronting suicidal feelings of shame, abandonment and hostility with no one to whom to turn.

Multiple parenting was an important cultural resource through which community was learned and many aspects of cultural feeling and information transmitted. By it trust was not dependent on one person but invested in many: the community is an extension of primary relationship.

In the West a cult has grown up around maternal attachment and the concept of bonding(18). Though this has come in for some cool reassessment(82, 102), there has also recently been a resurgence of somewhat polemical writing purporting to be research based which attempts to *prove* that it is human and necessary for babies to get hooked on their solitary mother and she on them(58). Child development in Polynesia reveals this view to be ethnocentric.

For generations Polynesians have grown to look to, to look at, many people as parents, to get hooked into a kin-group, not onto an individual. All these parents are the substance of the family and in Polynesia the family is not just the backbone of society —the family is society.

CHAPTER *4*

Being Born Into a Golden World

> 'In Fiji there is great rejoicing all around (especially within the extended family) following the birth of a child. And so much warmth and affection are lavished on the newborn.'
>
> 'Burying the umbilical cord was meant as an assurance that the child would not search for it in later life. A child in the habit of ransacking drawers, baskets, etc. was usually considered to have a lost or misplaced pito, thus the searching.'
>
> 'The mother and the relatives will always massage the legs of the newborn baby. A beautiful woman must have good legs. Handsome boys must have good legs, too.'
>
> 'In Tonga the birth of a baby is a time for feasting. In most cases a pig is killed for feasting.'
>
> 'My grandmother was particularly indulgent to me and insisted that early childhood was a time for play. I remember as a preschool child spending long periods playing poker with her because she wanted a partner.'

With so many parents around it is no wonder that the newborn child enters a golden world of love and attention, of cuddles and concern, of constant interaction, support in someone's arms or lap. Given such a start in the world most people would be friendly since the world itself is a friendly place.

Geddes, writing some time ago of Deumba, Fiji, said he never saw a child in tears, never saw an adult thrash a young child and that parents disliked seeing any child made miserable(40). And in rural Fiji the scene has not changed(55).

Polynesians are frankly openly and unreservedly indulgent to little babies, at least until they can walk and talk. Early indulgence is a cultural rule. This is the case when a baby is born live and whole. In pre-modern conditions abortion was universal in Polynesian societies and infanticide was not infrequent. The neglect (often to death) of disabled newborns may seem strange in view of all that warmth, love and early indulgence. Yet there is no real contradiction. When things went wrong abortion and infanticide were a possible means of correction, never very common, always secret and indeed a way of ensuring that the loving and caring would be available to those who lived, were well formed and would grow.

Most people seem to agree that in present-day Polynesia children are desired and large families considered a sort of natural feature of the Polynesian way of life. Actually genealogies do not give evidence of large numbers of children surviving, but this may simply be because only those of kinship significance are remembered. However, there is ample evidence that if people wanted to limit family size, the means to do so was available. Three sets of techniques were employed: limitations on sexual intercourse, abortion and infanticide.

Though sexual activity among young people was not subject to great restriction, nowhere in Polynesia was pre-marital sex openly condoned. Levy reports that in Tahiti girls are usually sexually active by the age of 16(61); Mead(75) said the same thing for even younger girls in Samoa, though this statement has been contested(49). Malo points out that in traditional times a young Rotuman girl had a great deal of sexual freedom(71). Both Levy and Mead comment on the relative infertility of young female adolescents; ovulation may not accompany early menstruation but we do not suggest anyone should rely on this possibility as a contraceptive measure! Unwanted pregnancies are usually accommodated these days by adoption for which there is good traditional precedent(21). Male withdrawal seems to have once been a common form of fertility control in Tikopia(113) and in the Lau group in Fiji(111). It is probably less used now and elsewhere in Polynesia the very idea is almost unthinkable. Why would anyone want to do that! Levy mentions a Tahitian belief that frequently changing partners reduces the risk of pregnancy. Thompson found the same idea in Lau(111), Marshall in Rai'vavae(73). We do not know if such wishful thinking still persists but if it does it should be someone's job to correct it.

Generally there was little or no prohibition on sexual intercourse after a child was born. Lau is an exception(111). There would seem to have been in most Polynesian cultures an absence of any cultural rule on this matter. It was and is an individual matter.

Abortion, though infrequent, was everywhere available and probably still is. The Beagleholes report it for Pukapuka(7), Levy for Tahiti(61), Heuer for the New Zealand Maori(48) and the techniques appear to be very general. For most Polynesian societies there are reports of deep massage and manual pressure being used, neither of which is, medically speaking, likely to be very effective. In Tahiti, New Zealand, Lau and in Hawaii there are reports of herbs that produce abortion but whether these actually worked is unreported. For Tahiti, we have accounts of tightly binding the body of the pregnant woman, and also of inserting a grass stalk to damage the foetus and induce abortion(61). Both techniques were probably far more widespread but the knowledge of abortion techniques belonged to women and most of the ethnographers have been men. Missionary opposition attempted to stamp out abortion as a recourse available to anyone needing it. Where abortion was practised it was recognised that it should be undertaken before the fourth month, that is after the third menstruation had been missed. One Maori informant told us that any failure to menstruate led to the immediate assumption that a pregnancy had occurred so that abortion would usually be performed in the early stages of pregnancy.

The very word infanticide raises such strong emotions in the modern world that the fact of its ordinary acceptance in the past by most Polynesian cultures now gains little mention. Damaged, unhealthy or pre-term babies would simply be left to die; there was nothing else that could be done. Miscarried foetuses were regarded with fear and horror. By the time missionary influences had worked through the Pacific such practices were less likely to be acknowledged. Levy notes that female children were more likely to suffer this fate than males. While it may be that this was a conscious removal from the breeding pool of future mothers it more likely reflects a lower social value on females. Oliver reports that in traditional Tahiti between a quarter and a third of newborn live children were killed within a half hour of birth(85). Danielsson in a personal communication expressed doubts about the veracity of the missionary and travellers' tale accounts on which this is based and asked how anyone would ever know. In his view infanticide was limited to mis-mating outside of royal or chiefly class or pregnancies of specialised dancers. Under ordinary circumstances elsewhere such acts were of rather low frequency and rather private.

Firth's account of infanticide as a ritual injunction imposed in times of famine in Tikopia is dramatic but probably exceptional because it violates the major Polynesian pattern which is that control of fertility rests in the hands of the women and is a personal, private, even secret, matter(34). Where knowledge of such matters is hidden it is not a proper matter for community discussion or even of note. The ordinary authority of most Polynesian chiefs would not extend into an area of personal privacy of this kind nor was it generally necessary since abortive techniques were available.

Nowadays the idea of family limitation is starting to catch on around the Pacific, but slowly. In New Zealand and Hawaii the use of chemical contraception by Polynesian women is more an elite practice, the most usual means being tubal ligation when they have had enough of child bearing. Epeli Hau'ofa makes a passionate call for speedy population control in Tonga and though tubal ligation is also available there and probably increasing in popularity, it is unlikely that this will be applied early enough to achieve overall population stability(47). In Fiji the Indian population has responded to the family planning campaign there; native Fijians hardly at all. Overpopulation has led to pressures to migrate almost everywhere, though especially in the Tokelaus, American Samoa and the Cooks. Fiji and New Zealand are the exceptions here.

Obviously infanticide is no longer a possible means of population control. Religious overlay has inhibited the freedom of women to use abortion even though all Polynesian cultures had it once. Limitation on sexual intercourse has a poor track record among the human species generally. We just are not very good at that. Finding means of limiting families that Polynesians, *and especially males*, will accept and use should be a high policy priority everywhere, but particularly in those small island states whose economies are so limited and whose ecologies so fragile.

Children were valued not so much as individuals but as part of the community; they ensured its continuity. However, any woman or couple unable to conceive would be given children through adoption just as older couples past childbearing age would have the comfort of grandchildren to carry them through their final years. In this sense, children were taken for granted and desired as social security for old age.

In Fiji herbal treatment or visiting a healer is still quite usual in treating infertility and even in New Zealand a *tohunga* may be consulted for its eradication.

Just as pregnancy appears to have been an accepted part of a woman's life and rather matter of fact so also, in most of Polynesia, giving birth is regarded as natural, accompanied by little perception of danger or anxiety with pain expected to be brief(61). We have, however, first hand reports from New Zealand of Maori and Tokelauan women being left alone in labour in hospitals and screaming loudly in their distress. Clearly the cultural setting of birth plays a major role in determining whether it shall be a comfortable or horrible experience.

Both pregnancy and birth put heavy limitations on women. In Pukapuka, for example, there is a long list of forbidden practices and forbidden foods, all designed to protect the child and ensure its normal development. In Tonga a woman in pregnancy may not truss chickens for the *umu* or cut *tapa* cloth lest the child be born deformed. In Fiji nothing tight must be worn around the mother's neck lest the umbilical cord strangle the foetus. Also in Fiji, a mother must immediately make her pregnancy known to her family or she will be a danger to those around her who may become sick. If she cuts someone's hair while her pregnancy is concealed that person will grow bald; if she prepares food the eaters will take ill; if she cares for children they may become sick. Quite frequently, undesirable characteristics in the children are attributed to the mother having done something or not done something during the pregnancy. On the other hand the pregnant woman is expected to want extra food or special foods and her desires in this matter will usually be met(7, 61, 94, 111).

Birth is essentially a female matter but in a few instances men may be present and have a role to play. In Pukapuka, a priestly male (*tangata waka wanau*) got behind the woman and massaged her back and from one Waikato Maori we have a report that traditionally the woman sat astride the squatting male, facing forward, who assisted and supported her when she wished to bear down. It would seem, however, that the presence of males or any role for them during birth was not at all common in most Polynesian locations. Generally speaking, birth took place at home, and was women's business, but in some locations, if the birth was successful, mother and child would go to a special lying-in house(12).

Since the role of women in food production was often very important, she would return to normal tasks as soon as possible, sometimes in a matter of days as in Tahiti where she might return to the fields as little as two days after the birth. A Tongan mother, however, will stay in bed for many many days, even months. In traditional Maori society and in Pukapuka, a week to ten days was allowed, though Holmes reports for Samoa that a mother was allowed four months respite from agricultural duties and in Fiji one to four months is usual and a mother has lots of other help with the baby as well.

Throughout Polynesia, the placenta (in Maori, *whenua*) and the umbilical cord (*pito*) were either buried or placed in a sacred tree and often there was important ritual conducted over them. Unless this was done, the child's link with its birthplace would be impaired and later attributes of the child were often related to little details that occurred or failed to occur during these rituals. In Tonga warm water is poured over the *fonua* to prevent the child from catching cold. This tender little practice has the quality of thoughtful attentive care that characterises the golden years of early life.

In most parts of Polynesia there was a traditional acknowledgment of the child with incantations, anointing with pure water or coconut oil, and often both mother and child were ritually massaged for some time following the birth, though not as extensively or for as long as on the Micronesian island of Palau where both are constantly so attended for as much as three weeks.

The birth often signifies the occasion for a feast on Pukapuka, Samoa and Tonga and probably elsewhere too. In Lau, the birth of a first child was celebrated with a bigger feast than subsequent births. Such feasts were often followed by the distribution of food to family and friends in Pukapuka (as is usual everywhere in Polynesia after a feast), and by the ritual exchange of gifts between the extended familes of the mother and the father in Samoa.

There seems to be, to us, a charming freedom about the giving of names to very young children. We suspect this may be because a child who survived infancy would sometimes be more seriously renamed after an appropriate ancestor after there had been time for the matter to be discussed. Also, until the survival of a child was assured there might be little incentive to invest it with a powerful traditional name. In Pukapuka the father generally named the child, but the mother or others could also contribute a name, so that a child could have different names in different groups. Naming needed time to settle down. A child could be renamed for relatives who died about the time it was born or for almost any other event occurring at the time. There was no sex distinction in names on Pukapuka, and no class of words set aside for exclusive use as personal names. A child could be named after an event, for example, tidal wave or big winds, a visitor (Miti

Moa, derived from Mr More, a missionary) or refer to a special skill or attribute of the father. In Maori society, whatever the given name, the child may be so commonly known by a nickname that the original name may come as rather a personal shock when he or she goes to school and is enrolled under the registered name. In Tonga, Aoyagi reports that the name is generally given by either the father or that very important father's sister, and first born children, in particular, were named by paternal relations(2). Special visitors might be given the privilege of choosing a name for the child. In Fiji a father names the first three and the mother the next three. Holmes lists various categories of names used in Samoa: natural (e.g. pigeon, butterfly, wind), compound names (e.g. go with love, it's better to come to the hospital), biblical names, and names deriving from events occuring at the time of the birth. He also mentions names of European influence such as telephone, kerosene and kleenex(49). Throughout Polynesia, there is nothing stereotyped about naming! Currently in Tonga Sekimeti has popularity as a female name, segment being one of the more charming concepts of the curriculum of new maths.

In this way, we think, the sanctity and specialness of the individual is less emphasised than in some other cultures when the business of naming is a matter of great sacred and sometimes even secret significance. In traditional times a childhood name would be abandoned at adulthood, or at any significant time in life a new name would be adopted to reflect a new status or maturing.

Whatever the traditional situation may have been, these days the young child in most Polynesian cultures will be breastfed for only three to four months (though in Tonga for at least double that time and up to a year). This is about the time when, in Samoa, the mother was expected to resume her full duties in the gardens. During this time she would be away from the child for from six to eight hours. Women do not usually breastfeed the child of another, as is often the case in Melanesia, but would pacify the child with coconut milk or other solid food. However, weaning is generally gradual because, throughout early infancy, everyone around the young child enjoys contact with it and its responsiveness to attention. Increasingly bottles and prepared baby foods gain favour. In the tropical Pacific artificial feeding is a real health hazard and needs to be actively discouraged. Indeed, the recent decision in Papua New Guinea that bottle feeding be banned will do no one any harm except the marketers of bottles and artificial foods.

Let us look a little further at the topic of nutrition. There is no doubt that all is not well in respect of the nourishment of the pregnant mother(88). In a recent New Zealand study there was clear evidence of a high rate of Maori children born with small heads(46). Foetal undernourishment leads to poor development of neural tissue; brains starved at vital times in their growth can never make up lost ground(61).

Children are also vulnerable to malnutrition at later ages, and especially at weaning. McKenzie reports, for the Cook Islands, that 80 per cent of pre-school children were anaemic(70). In a later study, 2143 children were examined (a 99 per cent sample) and only fifteen of them were diagnosed healthy. This is not evidence of the gross malnutrition of Asia and Africa, of kwashiorkor or mirasmus, but an undetected general lowering of effort, energy and functioning through borderline nutrition. In such circumstances when disease strikes children may die.

Where children must eat in order of status precedence in the household (visitors first, adult men next, other adults and adolescents and women and *then* the children), they may have to survive on scraps or if fed it will be on taro or cassava or other carbohydrate with very low protein value. Also, junk food has washed into the Pacific as elsewhere with its low food values, sugar addiction and dangerous ease.

Holmes thinks that little Samoan babies are overdressed; in contrast, Pukapukan babies wore nothing at all. Certainly in most parts of modern Polynesia parents will go to great lengths, particularly on public occasions, to show that they are good parents who care by dressing the child in Western-type baby clothes and in the case of girls, the frillier and the prettier the better, especially for Sunday church or special occasions such as a marriage.

Toilet training is accomplished without much fuss, geared pretty much to the child's own pace and physical control. No one in Polynesia could appreciate the fuss Westerners once made about it—especially psychoanalysts.

All those who have written about Polynesian childhood agree that universally it is a time of great attention and affectionate display. Here is Howard's account of early childhood in Hawaii:

> During infancy, youngsters are attended to very closely. Much of their waking time is passed in someone's arms, being cuddled, played with, and talked to. At family gatherings it is common practice for an infant to be passed from one to another; holding

a baby is perceived as a privilege rather than a responsibility, so that age takes precedence. Usually it is the older women who monopolize a child, although over a period of time almost everyone—even teenage boys who may like to come on 'tough' at times—is apt to be given an opportunity to indulge in fondling, looking at, and pacifying an infant. Although men, on the average, spend less time holding and cuddling an infant, the pleasure they display when they do appears no less intense than the delight shown by women. At no time did we hear any male chide another for giving attention to an infant, nor did we obtain any evidence that to do so is unmasculine. Quite the contrary—some of the hardest drinking, belligerent men openly showed the greatest tenderness. An infant is rarely allowed to cry for more than a few seconds before someone comes to provide relief. Mothers are pressured to do so; if a child is left crying other persons present show signs of distress. Speculations are made as to the cause of the baby's discomfort and other indirect cues are emitted to let the mother know that if she does not attend to the child's welfare immediately she is likely to be branded negligent. Consistent with this pattern is the practice of demand feeding. Although a few women reported attempts to establish a feeding schedule, they were almost invariably given up within a few days; the cries of a hungry baby were just too much to bear. Feeding an infant is more than just a means of providing nourishment, however. It has symbolic value in the sense that it provides a public display of nurturance, or concern for the child's welfare. Food was therefore offered to crying infants even when it seemed clear to field workers that the child was not hungry, but distressed for other reasons. There were even some reports of infants being fed when their distress was more than likely the result of overeating(51, pp. 40–41).

The child is received not just into the arms of a loving mother but into a wide circle of people of all ages and both genders among whom it is a welcome new member of the family, a household member, a part of the kinship network and a member of the community. In Tahiti the act of parenting is termed *whanau* which means to deliver a child, to father a child, or to bear a child. The same word is used affectionately and inclusively among the New Zealand Maori to wrap people up in the idea that all those present at a gathering who acknowledge their descent from a common ancestor are as though one large family. So a child is not born to parents; it is born from parents to the *whanau*.

Everyone is delighted when a new child is born except perhaps the child next oldest in age, if there is one. But even here there is the cultural mechanism whereby sibling rivalry is translated later into status rivalry and becomes an acceptable part of Polynesian life. This we will discuss later.

Western observers looking at this very early period of infancy, in the case of every Polynesian culture which has been reported in the anthropological literature, emphasise how unrestrained is the warmth and love with which the child is surrounded. When they use words like indulgence this is perhaps because, compared with their own childhood, the frank and open way in which adults and older children enjoy little children, meeting their every need, is undoubtedly enviable. Culturally speaking, we know of no area in the world that is warmer and more accepting of tiny babies than is Polynesia.

Westerners are afraid of 'spoiling' their children, a term derived from the biblical expression 'save the rod and spoil the child'. Their tradition emphasises the need to restrain and discipline a child from the beginning—a hangover from the Judeo–Christian and Calvinist past, the conception that a human being is born in sin and must be redeemed. Though few Westerners today believe in that theology many inhibit their natural response to little ones. All that seems very strange to Polynesians who have no belief in the value of scheduling feedings and sleeping times, nor of the necessity for a small child to sleep in a separate crib or cot.

Nowadays of course, not all Polynesian babies are surrounded by the aunts and cousins, nieces and nephews, grandparents and uncles and fathers, and working back to this cultural ideal may require some effort in redesigning urban life. But the satisfactions and the rewards are too great, we think, for this departure from a culturally desirable way to be anything other than temporary. For those for whom childhood was like this there likely are residual memories of how wonderful that state was. That kind of memory anyone would seek to recapture.

CHAPTER 5

Early Independence

> 'I often cringe to myself when I see a mother disciplining a young child with slaps or with a broom of coconut frond mid-ribs and I remember inwardly some of the punishments I had as a youngster.'
>
> 'I can just about feel the pain that befalls the youngsters growing up.'
>
> 'In my childhood I experienced whippings and threats that the ghosts will get you. This I think affected me a great deal in my early childhood and adolescence because I was very frightened to go out alone at night, even to walk from one end of the village to another.'
>
> 'I remember when I was a child I could swim before I was 6. My mother didn't teach me to swim. By the time I went to school I acted quite independently. By the time I was 8 I could go out for reef fishing when it was low tide.'
>
> 'Very early in life children in my island have freedom to wander around the whole island and very rarely do you see parents going around looking for their children. In many cases they miss their meals and the only meal they would not miss is the evening meal.'

As we have been, so to speak, building the house of childhood in Polynesia we laid the floor of community, raised the corner posts of multiple parenting, lashed on the framework of early warmth and indulgence. Now on goes the roof: early in life children are allowed to be, expected to be, remarkably autonomous and to grow progressively in independence from the age of two or even earlier.

In this chapter we shall examine what it is that Polynesian parents expect in this regard, how children respond to their expectations and what the consequences are.

At birth, the immediate, urgent biological problem is how will an infant so tiny, weak and helpless survive. Survival can never be taken as guaranteed. For Raroia, Danielsson reported that out of seventy-five live births, seventeen children died in infancy; that is a 22 per cent death rate and there is still that perilous first year of life ahead(27). Even without temporary disasters such as cyclones or drought, in Anuta almost every household had experienced at least one infant death(118). McArthur reports even higher figures for Tonga and Samoa(65). For the island of Kauai, in the Hawaiian group, of each 1000 pregnancies, 237 ended without a live birth and a further fourteen per thousand died within a month of birth(116). That is a total of 25 per cent. Much of this infant mortality is related to poor nutrition during pregnancy. Even in New Zealand there has been no appreciable reduction in Maori infant mortality rates in the last decade(112).

Around the world people from all cultures anxiously take whatever steps they can to prevent early mortality and to ensure survival and this is basically a biological matter. Culture plays some part but until the child is firmly on the track of life it is biological and ecological rather than cultural influences which are most important. Still, as we have seen, the cultural response in Polynesia to survival threat in young children is to be lavish in attention and almost boundlessly loving and indulgent. This child may be the one that does not survive; love it while you can. The same kind of pattern occurs in reports of the New Zealand Maori(9, 92, 94, 97), for Hawaii(38, 52), Pukapuka(7), Raroia(26) and Tahiti(61).

But in every case, what the Beagleholes call the golden years come to an end. Survival assured, culture intervenes and the pattern of the Polynesian character begins to be formed.

In writing about this some of the observers have used the strong psychologically loaded term 'rejection' and so before we look at the field reports we should examine the concept of rejection itself. It is now our assertion that this term is altogether too strong and too severe to describe what is taking place. Rather we are dealing with an early and quite deliberate cultural act of socialisation which is better described as the early beginnings of an independence that is culturally desired and carefully fostered. The consequences of this, as we will see, are quite different from those we would expect either theoretically or on the basis of research on rejection.

Rohner defines rejection as a parent–child relationship characterised by an absence of warmth and affection, frequent and severe physical punishment and hostility towards the child(101). In Palau, not a Polynesian island, rejection is severe and obvious(4). The mother, by deliberate act and decision, one day withdraws love, affection and attention from the child who is left to cope as best it may. Among the Alorese in Indonesia there is a similar sharp and deliberate discontinuity at about the age of two(30). The mother one day just walks away. From these and similar societies Rohner concludes that early rejection results in pernicious and malignant effects. Adults who were rejected as children are hostile and aggressive, dependent, emotionally unresponsive, have negative views about themselves, other people and the world in general. They are emotionally unstable and even view the gods as hostile. Every now and again one may meet a Polynesian who is like this but this is not a pattern for the whole area or for any of its cultures.

When is rejection likely to be present? From Rohner's cross-cultural survey data the answer is when mothers are unremittingly bound to the children and unable to accept the constancy and intensity of their demands. Rejection is less likely when fathers help with the children, or when there are grandparents or others who are 'significantly nurturant agents'. When the working role of mothers is heavy so that they have little time or energy left to care for their children, you can expect rejection. Furthermore, around the world, parents who indulge their babies are prone to go on nurturing their children. Adults who were accepted as children (the opposite of rejection) show more generosity and responsibility. They view the world and the gods as benevolent and tend to be cheerful and expressive.

Now, if this is what rejection means and implies, are the accounts of rejection in Polynesian childrearing justified? We think not. All the indicators point in the opposite direction. It is more than just a stereotype that Polynesians are cheerful and happy. Throughout Polynesia both traditional and contemporary religious beliefs view the world of the supernatural as of great solace, comfort, support and aid to human actions. Interpersonal relations are not hostile; caretaking is shared and motherhood is not constant and unremitting, or at least used not to be though it may be becoming more so now.

What then were the ethnographers, including ourselves, talking about? If you separate the reports of behaviour from the comments on it the accounts are referring to a change both in the behaviour of children and in the attitudes of those around the children which occurs at about the second year of life, or perhaps earlier if another child arrives sooner than this. The child receives a strong cultural message that infancy is over and the road to maturity has begun.

52 Growing up in Polynesia

The message also states that the child must now turn for attention not just to adults who may indeed ignore his or her requests, but to other children, and this is the beginning of learning what community is about. It is also a message about the cultural distinction between the serious world of adult concerns and the rather carefree world of childhood. This message contains the idea that adults and parents have other things to do than simply attend to children's wants. The democratic nature of Polynesian institutions demands a high degree of sensitivity in balancing personal wishes against community acceptance and needs. To gain this degree of sensitivity the training of independence must be begun early. There is a long way to go. There is much to be learned. From both a parental and an adult point of view a person whose dependency needs are over-promoted and under-socialised will not be an adequate Polynesian personality.

The particular nature of the induction of the child into this new aspect of its life has a different flavour in each of the Polynesian cultures and to appreciate this we must really direct you to a detailed reading of the separate cultural accounts. But we can illustrate them by some quotations and research summaries. Gallimore, Boggs and Jordan report for Hawaii:

> Pumehana infants are indulged by both adults and older children and a frequent focus of positive parental attention, but they experience fairly dramatic changes as they leave infancy. As they learn to walk and talk, and as other infants displace them from the 'baby' position in the household, they begin to experience quite different demands and expectations. They seem to be re-categorized and their status shifted from 'baby' to 'child', with an accompanying change in associated roles. The 'shift' usually occurs around the age of two, but varies with individual family structure and other circumstances. For example, the 'baby' position may be filled by a new infant who in effect displaces the former occupant. Under some circumstances, a toddler without a younger rival may remain in the 'baby' role well beyond the age of two, although even in these cases a visiting infant will temporarily change its status . . . An infant that cries and fusses until picked up, fed, changed, and so on is acceptable; a whining, clinging, demanding toddler is not. While babies live in the midst of an adult world, indeed, often at its very center, children are expected to function in a separate sphere that only overlaps that of adults at the peripheries. To

a large extent, they are not to intrude into adult activities except on invitation, or if they must have adult assistance, they should request it in a subtle and unobtrusive fashion, marking the presence of a need without making demands to which an adult must respond. In part, the stereotype of Pumehana mothers as rejecting or indifferent is based on the firmness with which they deal with intrusions on occasions when they seemed inappropriate. Commands to 'go out', 'go play', 'go sistah' and 'stop crying', and swats and threats of swats were all frequently observed(38, pp. 118–120).

Notice that these authors speak of the 'stereotype of rejection'. Westerners looking from the outside at Polynesian adults handling the behaviour of children who are at this stage see their actions as harsher than they are or are intended to be. And often they notice the contrast with adult behaviour towards younger children too. But Polynesian adults are not rejective—merely firm.

Here is another account from Hawaii:

Once the point of change has been reached, children are no longer the indulged center of attraction they were as infants. They are removed to the fringes of the adult world, and much of the attention they receive is in the form of demands ('Go get me a glass of water') or admonishments ('Stop bothering me'). Thus children are faced with their initial strategic challenge—how to regain the indulgent rewards of their previously favored status. Quite naturally, they rely on the tactics that paid off so handsomely before. They cry, whine, tug on parental clothing, try to climb into adult laps and otherwise attempt to take central stage in the social arena. These tactics may pay off some of the time during the transition period, and may therefor be perpetuated for a while, but they also draw increasingly harsh punishment(51, p. 41).

Howard's explanation for the change is in terms of social status. He thinks that children are at the bottom of the pecking order and that by being harsh parents are teaching their children to respect rank. Certainly we would agree that throughout Polynesia parents regard it as important that children will learn respect because, as we will discuss later, status rivalry is limited or contained by the restraint of respect which is such an important cultural trait that the teaching of it should be begun as soon as possible. Furthermore, respect for age is *the* most important kind in cultures that make respect of many kinds a continuous and conspicuous obligation. But we doubt that Howard is right in this explanation. Respect is not the only reason for the shift in parental attitude and the teaching of respect may well be an effect rather than a cause.

The change comes in the life of New Zealand Maori children in much the same way, as this account shows:

> Infancy is over. The child is on its own but it is difficult to see any consistent pattern of behaviour held out as acceptable to the child. It is almost as though the parents were saying, 'Well, the sooner the child is left to mature like old wine the better, and the less interference with it the quicker the process will be'. Adult action is a world apart; a world which permits no interference from active children except as adults bid. The helplessness and novelty of new babies is interesting to adults but the activities of toddlers merely immature and best ignored. Actual remonstrations of very young children are decidedly rare in records of observation. Usually very young children would be placed on the floor and left to their own devices. If they interfered with the adults they might be picked up and dandled for a short time and then put back. If they still cried or objected then an older child would be called to take them away. On occasions a child might be cuffed for continued attempts at attracting attention.
>
> Indulgence is not immediately withdrawn for all time as soon as the child can toddle. But after this time it is dependent upon the whim of adults and the reactions of the adult world become unpredictable . . . Parents are not, however, harsh or punitive in the way in which they separate themselves from their young children. The infant no longer receives the same attention or care as before. Though he may suffer from an occasional off-handed slap, nothing is comparable to the deep resentment which characterises the rejecting parent in the literature of clinical psychology. Furthermore, the child is not bound by a close, emotionally ambivalent relationship within the constant company of busy parents but is simply placed outside the door where siblings must act as surrogate parents to the best of their ability and patience(92, p. 238).

Here is an actual field record of how parent and child interact at about this stage:

Early Independence

David is entertaining his wife's father and his sister's husband in the living room–kitchen of their house. His six sons are playing 'bulldozers' in the dusty part of the backyard and from time to time you can hear sounds of their play through the open window. David is discussing an offer made by a local logging contractor for part of his wife's family's bush and has got deeply into the complexities of royalties and lawyers. His wife is preparing afternoon tea and cooking the evening meal at the same time as she carries the youngest baby on the crook of her left arm. David's next eldest enters the kitchen and goes to his mother who goes on with her work and ignores the child. Comes over to his father and tries to climb on his knee. Father pushes him off. Goes over to the open space in front of the fire and begins circling around, quite rapidly on the one spot. Mother crossing to tend cooking brushes him into a corner. After mother leaves fire child goes to fire and takes out burning stick. Mother goes and removes stick. Child urinates. Mother calls second eldest child and assigns the other to his care. Both children go outside. Later same child enters with the next eldest. At this point there was a break in the conversation as the story of the negotiations had been completed and both children climbed on to the sofa next to their father and grandfather and begin a hand slapping game. Afternoon tea interrupts and both children are sent off outside without further ado(92, p. 239).

Surprisingly Lowell Holmes does not comment on the shift in parental attitudes and behaviour for Samoa even though it is there in his description(49). He mentions that in the first four or five months, the child 'is nursed whenever it cries, it is constantly attended to, rocked to sleep at night and showered with love and affection' (p. 76). But later,

> Attempts at early training are often accompanied by severe punishment. Erring children are sometimes slapped on the buttocks, legs, or face or switched on the legs or buttocks with brooms made of coconut leaf midribs or even with leather belts. Mothers usually administer the punishment, although belt whippings of older children by fathers is not uncommon. Threats that the *aitu* (ghosts) 'will get you' are sometimes made, but the common deterrent to improper behaviour is refusing to allow children to go out and play in the moonlight when all the other children are doing so. While youngsters may be reprimanded for making too much noise or for standing in the house, little

is said about the very common practice of throwing stones or bullying smaller youngsters. Parents often resort to stone throwing themselves; a crying baby may receive a shower of small pebbles accompanied by shouts of '*Soia!*' ('Stop it!'), '*Uma!*' ('Enough!'), or '*Filemu!*' ('Peace!')(49, p. 78).

Levy echoes the same theme for Tahiti but draws out a different aspect of parental motivation:

> As they begin to become more and more children rather than babies, and begin to be a bit irritating and willful because they are 'thinking for themselves', people begin to find children less amusing. Instead of being the centre of the household stage, the child whose bids for attention were responded to, encouraged, and, in fact, taught, becomes annoying. He is now too old to show off, to 'inflate' himself. The child is now, perhaps, between three and five years old. 'He wants to play more outside the house', one is told, and he is encouraged to do so. Often another baby is born or adopted about this time but even if it is not, the child is now defined as something different. This has been described for other Polynesian and Micronesian cultures as 'rejection'. More accurately, the child's desire for certain kinds of interactions is now no longer 'indulged'. This involves for the most part two kinds of activities: those involving showing off, being cocky, amusing, and exhibitionist, and those related to dependency and clinging. Dependent and clinging activities have been discouraged in subtle ways even before this period, but now the pressure against them is increased. Exhibitionist activities, however, have been encouraged. The child is now to be relatively ignored(61, pp. 454–455).

For Raroia we do not have the same detailed information but Danielsson emphasises that at about the age of three, children may be set to do adults' work and at this same time they are expected to behave in an adult way(26, 27).

It is constructive to compare the Polynesian way of initiating independence training and the carrying of it through at this relatively early age with what goes on in the European family in New Zealand(97). In the latter case, independence is delayed, both because the highly independent child might create difficulties of control for the parent in a highly hazardous environment and because the role of the child is intimately linked with that of the mother. Indeed, it is through maintaining child dependency that she validates her role. Polynesians have houses but they do not have housewives.

Polynesian women, without exception, have an important role in economic production; often they are also involved in social and political organisation, in running the village as well as the home and the gardens, in taking produce to market, in teaching crafts, dance and chant. In fact, there are very few cultures in the world where a woman's role is specialised for child minding and little else. That is a peculiar Western aberration and recent at that. As Margaret Mead said, what Western people think of as *their* traditional family was actually invented in the last twenty-five years! Even during World War II many women worked, as they do in most cultures. The evidence also suggests that when women's roles are limited to house and family the effects are bad for both women and children(13, 14, 98). In fact, as we will see, the women in Polynesia are altogether too busy and socially involved for them to turn inward on their children in this way. And where families are larger, and Polynesian families, even in New Zealand, are larger than the European, the same intense one-to-one form of socialisation and maternal scrutiny and vigilance is simply not possible. The European concept of individualism requires quite a different kind of independence training from the Polynesian concept of collectivism.

Just in passing, for we will discuss this more fully later, we should note that this is one reason why it is dangerous uncritically to attempt to transplant some such institution as the European pre-school or kindergarten into a Polynesian setting—the whole elaborate model on which it is based is different, both in terms of the child's character and the maternal role.

Let us then lay to rest the ethnocentric value judgment implied in the use of the term rejection. When Gallimore, Boggs, and Jordan speak of the 'shift' and Levy speaks of 'distancing', they were certainly not referring to the regular clinical connotation of rejection. Whatever the term used, this customary way of treating children around the age of two is a culture pattern—another major theme in Polynesian socialisation. The first is the surrounding community within which growing up occurs. The second is the world of many parents. The third is the richness of all that love and attention that surrounds the young child. The fourth is this progression towards autonomy and competence by which the child learns to depend on many and balance that dependency with a sense of autonomy and independence. If Polynesians were to give this up they would indeed be in danger of losing their inheritance.

There is a very simple explanation of why this shift occurs and it rests on unconscious assumptions in the minds of Polynesian people about how infancy should be, what adult behaviour should be and how, through childhood and socialisation, one makes the transition. The Western way is to overlap the model of being a child and that of adult behaviour so that, ideally, the first becomes lessened and the second becomes greater, progressively, over the twenty years of growing up. The Polynesian view is not like that at all.

In Polynesia there are three clear divisions in growing up: infancy, childhood and adulthood. The boundaries are more or less clear, not fuzzy or blurred. The transitions across them are marked by clear cultural changes, ceremonies, practices or *rites de passage*. Even though the break between infancy and childhood is not a matter of ritual, it is still a matter of custom. You can not put a definite age to it. Nor is it set for every child at the same age. Parents have discretion. But it is a definite transition just the same. As we will see, the transition from childhood to adulthood is more definitely and often ritually marked and recognised. But the absence of ritual does not mean that this earlier transition (from infancy to childhood) is any the less customary—that is, there are universally expected ways in which the cultural concepts of infancy and childhood are expressed in behaviour and their boundaries marked by transition.

A custom expresses cultural values. A ritual merely makes more clear that a custom exists and has authority. What are the customary values which Polynesians express when they alter their parental behaviour towards very young children? In our view, as we have stated earlier, the central value is that individuality should always be seen against a collective background, that independence should never be expressed without acknowledging dependency. This cultural message is of such profound importance to all aspects of Polynesian life that it becomes one of the earliest messages that children must receive, and receive it they do. In Polynesian society you may not leave the people behind. On the other hand, if you recognise this, the people are always there, with you, supporting you.

Howard and Gallimore tussled with the problem of early independence training(52). They designed an ingenious set of social psychological experiments to test or show how inhibited

Early Independence   59

Polynesian children become over the expression of dependent feelings. They thought that independence training was simply the inhibition of appeals for help to others. They were baffled by the fact that they could find little evidence for direct independence training in the contemporary Hawaiian household. But the evidence that they were looking for was in terms of direct reward for acting independently (which is the way Westerners are thought to develop independence in their children), or punishment for acting dependently, and for that they found considerable evidence. Howard at one point, discussing the reluctance of Hawaiian children to ask for help in one of their experiments, suggests that while verbal requests were inhibited, the children may have been signalling for help in non-verbal help ways that the experimentors did not recognise. Maybe so, but it is also possible that Hawaiian children have learned to look elsewhere for help than to adults and that their feelings of independence are best expressed and most supported when they are among their peers. That is to say, they have already learned the Polynesian message that one seeks help here, but not there, that there is a time to show dependency and a time to be independent, that in Polynesia the mix of dependency and independence is balanced and situational and must be measured against who you are with and where you are. We think that is what Polynesian children are learning when Polynesian parents shift their attitude towards them.

Infancy is over then (but its memory is not). The child is now a child in childhood. There are new developmental tasks to be mastered.

CHAPTER 6

Children Together

'At the age of ten I was left in the care of my aunt and uncle while my parents were away from home for about three months. As there were many girls of a similar age, I did not miss my parents.'

'Saturdays we all spent gathering vegetables from the bush for the Sunday meals. Firewood collecting was also our task. While the adults got together for a village gathering, e.g. a meeting or a church conference, the younger children were left in our care.'

'Girls are expected to stay closer to home. In this way they are expected to look after the younger ones.'

'There are very few entertainments in which the children could participate. Becuase of this, children tend to form groups. They sometimes sing songs, recite poetry, and play at wrestling. They expect adults not to interfere with their activities but sometimes the older folks chase them away because of the great noise they make.'

'Now as I sit back and try to recall my early days I find that it is very hard to believe it. At almost midnight we were still out from our homes. Some of us were very young, and yet our parents did not worry about our whereabouts.'

'Like other children in my village, I used to fetch water from the village well almost every morning and every evening. I was also introduced at an early age to such activities as helping adults make copra, feeding chickens and pigs, and sometimes cooking. I also had time to play such games as marbles, chasing, hide and seek with boys of my own age.'

'When I was in my later childhood, I was given the responsibility to look after my two younger sisters and my younger brother when my mother was away from home.'

'I grew up in the town, but when I made a visit back home, I used to go out with my cousins to collect coconuts or go fishing. It seemed like I was really a "city softie" because my cousins could collect more coconuts than I could. On fishing trips, these cousins would again show me up with their fishing skills by catching more

fish than I could. But it seemed that these children understood how I felt, as they would assure me not to worry and would share out their catch or their coconuts with me in order to trick the adults in the village into thinking that I was not all that bad.'
'The life of a youngster in Samoa seems to be rough on the surface. Behind that there is also a lot of fun play acting etc., in the bush while fetching coconuts, or in the free-for-all games in the lagoon, beach or hide and seek at night. Oh, those were the days!!!'

Now that the major themes of early childhood have been made clear, it is time to consider how the framework of our symbolic house of childhood shall be finished. It is clad, so to speak, with the thatch and walls of companionship; it is the company and friendship of other children (siblings and peers in the terminology of child development) that wraps the child around and gives comfort and security against the chills and winds of childhood. It is other children that close the walls of experience within which one may have fun and feel complete and quietly rest.

There is no doubt that the impact of emotional loss that might possibly occur when Polynesian parents decide for each child that infancy is over is lessened because, typically, Polynesians live in communities and children can turn to each other or to other adults for social and emotional support. Unlike the Western nuclear family where such an abrupt discontinuity would leave the child in a social and emotional vacuum, the extended family, the allocation of responsibility to older children and the support of other children, the linkage of such families in community, provide social and cultural resources through which Polynesian children learn to be Polynesian.

The general context of childhood in such communities is in the company of children and in many ways this is recognised. When children enter an adult context of ceremony or meetings, at church, or even in more casual settings of entertainment, they do so on adult terms. Outside and all about, always available, is the other world of children. It is not cut off from the adult world but continuously lies alongside it. Even though they are inhabiting the same single-room dwelling, children and adults are living different lives.

In the past, this was formally recognised in some Polynesian cultures by the provision of boys' clubs and girls' clubs, and sometimes separate sleeping houses at adolescence. Nowadays, this is less likely to be the case, but whether or not these are formal groups, single sex peer groups are found everywhere and are a powerful and important part of Polynesian life and childhood.

The link between the two worlds is more or less formally guided by the responsibilities which parents place on children firstly to look after themselves, secondly to look after each other, thirdly to look after a special younger child and finally to contribute to the running of a household through regular tasks. In the course of performing these activities which link their lives with those of other children significant cultural messages are received and learned.

Back in 1930 Margaret Mead commented on the adultlike role of pre-adolescent girls in Samoa in caring for younger children(75) and Holmes' more recent study confirms the continuation of this widespread practice(44). The Beagleholes did not mention it for Pukapuka(7), nor for their study of the New Zealand community which they called Kowhai(9), but we certainly found it in Rakau where even quite young children had responsibility for their younger brothers and sisters(91, 92, 94). Other field workers who have looked at childhood among the New Zealand Maori have remarked on it(77). It is even recognised in the language which provides different words for an elder sibling (*tuakana*) and for a younger (*teina*). The modern Hawaiian material explores this matter in considerable depth(38). Levy, writing of Tahiti, mentions it and he stresses that there are a large number of people who act in a parental relationship with the child(61). Howard, however, does not report children as caretakers of infants on Rotuma(51). Indeed, this is a major difference because while older siblings have the right to direct the activities of younger siblings, and boys to act as their sisters' guardians, there is more emphasis on interpersonal respect in childhood and a greater degree of direct modelling on adult people who act in a parental way. Rotuma is rather different from the rest of Polynesia in the way that independence and achievement are patterned.

For Raroia, Danielsson reports:

> Children begin to have certain duties at the age of three. The Raroians' view is that the children, like all the other members of the family, ought to make themselves useful, and they give even quite small children astonishingly heavy and difficult tasks. Children of four or five are sent regularly to fetch water from the large communal tank; many of them do as many as ten trips a day with their gallon bottles. Others are set to grate

coconuts, wash up or do other kitchen work. A girl of eight washes, irons and cooks, while a boy of the same age helps to make copra or is sent out fishing. At about the same age many girls begin to look after their younger brothers and sisters, which does not mean just that they are told to keep an eye on them now and then, but that they have also to wash, dress and occupy them—in other words, entirely replace the parents. It is quite usual, too, for a boy or girl to be left behind in the village with a solitary grandmother to keep house when the family goes to the islands in the lagoon for several weeks to make copra(26, p. 121).

This practice of child caretakers, while it is not exclusive to Polynesia, is something which the general literature of child development appears to have overlooked almost entirely. Gallimore and his associates point out that the *Handbook of Socialization Theory and Research*, which has over 1000 pages, does not discuss any other person taking care of children except parents(38). Indeed, in Western societies, the degree of child caretaking that seems to apply in most of Polynesia would probably be regarded as child neglect and viewed with some horror. There are two reasons for this. One is the extreme danger to young children that has been created by the environment of Western technology and the other is the Western theory of human nature which implies that children are not to be trusted—and certainly not with the total care of other children. Western society still believes that children are imperfect adults. In Polynesia, children are children, and so there is no reason at all not to trust older children with the care of younger.

Also, since all relatives of the same generation as the mother have effective parental roles—and the same is often true for the relatives of the father—the responsibility of the biological parents is further reduced. This fact is further revealed by the high incidence of adoption and fostering. While everybody knows who their real parents are, parenting is a community function, allocated to biological parents, to adult relatives, to adolescents, and even to children who are but a few years older than the child for whom they have parenting responsibilities and duties. Thus the growing child can turn to many resource people and need not depend on only one or two. There is security in this, safety, someone to turn to, a whole world on which to depend if need be, so that the need is hardly noticed, so readily is it met.

Boys are less involved in sibling caretaking but they too may be called upon to play their role and far from there being any disgrace in doing so, they may earn commendation for it. Like their sisters, they may be assigned to the care of one special child exclusively and Gallimore notes that in Hawaii older children will be made responsible not only for general care and supervision of a particular younger child, but once they are working they also have economic responsibilities to provide for that child's material needs—toys, clothes, educational necessities(38).

It makes a difference to the whole of one's later development if the person who is giving rewards and punishments to the child is only a few years older than that child. Weisner and Gallimore have picked up the challenge of exploring this difference in a paper that looks at sibling caretaking on a world scale(117). They encountered several problems. When an ethnography does not mention the matter, is that because there is no sibling caretaking or because the matter has not been noted? But even when it is mentioned, studies usually focus on maternal caretaking. Theories of child development generally imply that the child is the passive recipient of the care one adult gives him or her, and ignore, as we have already noted, the pervasiveness of sibling caretaking as well as the effects which children may have on those who take care of them, whoever they may be.

Weisner and Gallimore hypothesise that child caretaking by siblings will reduce or dilute the saturation and force or intensity of parent socialisation and in particular lessen attachment to the mother. On her part the attachment may not so much be lessened as become latent. A Samoan friend writes: 'She stands afar and takes pride or shame in her children's interactions with their peers . . . this may be expressed to her friends in private or to the child when no one else is around.' Parental socialisation does continue but is less directly, publicly and openly expressed. Thus instead of childhood seeming like a staircase with fixed and regular intervals and regular progression towards the goal of adult status, childhood is a world of equals. Child caretaking and peer socialisation certainly affects the nature and organisation of play groups as well as their sex composition. It dilutes the specialness and individuality of the particular family into which the child was born so that family and community became almost identical. It provides the development of pro-social, nurturant and responsible behaviour both in the children who mind and the children who are minded, for they too one day will mind. Where the caretaking tasks are assigned differently to boys and girls the load is likely to fall more heavily on the girls so that societies in which there is considerable child caretaking by other children probably provide earlier and stronger sex role training for the girls. And at the same time, in that situation, boys are learning that child minding is not their role.

When Western children are given responsibility to mind others it is usually occasional, time specific and under adult scrutiny and ultimate responsibility. Often older children 'mind' younger ones, especially in rural areas, but the allocation is not so general or extensive. It is only a temporary parent substitute, not a way of life.

In personality terms, shared child caretaking probably reduces the development of individual differences. You just do not get the strong impact of a single character model. Children are more likely to be trained to become people like *us*, rather than a person like *me*. They are probably less likely to show the same traits and characteristics as their biological parents if suddenly the peer group becomes exposed to influences that parents can not resist. The situational nature of responsibility may be increased, that is, if I am not looking after the child, I can assume that somebody else is.

Weisner and Gallimore speculate that children raised in this situation are more field-dependent, that is, they require a great deal of information from the environment, especially the social environment, before they can act with assurance. It may also be true that children raised by other children have to depend more on non-verbal information than on verbal signals or cues for guidance as to the right way to act and appropriate behaviour. There seems to be some evidence that child caretaking develops affiliation motives and reduces individual achievement and the desire for it.

Again we find ourselves puzzled by the discrepancy between standard child development theory and the Polynesian case. The text book theory makes much of identifying with a parent model but we doubt that this is very important in Polynesian psychology. Both multiple parenting and peer socialisation make single parent modelling unlikely. We don't *know* that it does not occur. But we have doubts.

But of one thing we have no doubt. There is no evidence whatsoever that children suffer in any way when they are cared for by other children. And, since the parents' load is lessened, they are likely to be more easygoing and contented and thus make life easier for the children(78). Many hands make work lighter. We would also hypothesise that child caretaking leads to high levels of cultural complexity. Authoritarian leadership develops less complex social systems(1). It may be simpler to run the show when a single parent or two takes charge—but multiple parenting is bound to be more complex. Furthermore if children are running their show the parents may have more time to enjoy elaborate cultural complexities like the Samoan status system.

But the most profound effect of child caretaking is to distribute attachment to many people and many ages, so that for ever after the child will look toward the community as a distributed and distributing pattern of authority which must be understood.

What has been revealed by this aspect of growing up in Polynesia has enormous implications for understanding the distinctive nature of Polynesian culture. But beyond this, socialisation by other children is Polynesia's great gift to the literature of child development, for nowhere else do we find that the importance of sibling caretaking has even been recognised. If we were to rewrite Western manuals of child care we would put in some strong advice to the world in general and the Western world in particular. Sibling caretaking should be recognised, promoted and valued; it develops some valuable human attributes.

The pragmatism of Polynesia also comes through in the way other duties are allocated to children (apart from that of minding other children, important though this be). Since the family and the community need to be maintained and children are part of it, why should children not participate according to their capacities in those things that must be done for the household and community to run effectively? Therefore, Polynesian families give their children jobs to do and if sometimes parents and other caretakers sharply insist that they be done it is not only because if they are not, someone else will have to do them, but also because responsibility is to be shared and one must learn that it cannot be avoided.

Even when children have their own activities, like lagoon fishing, they are expected to share the catch—which on the face of it does not look like carrying out the garbage, but when you think about it, is. This is their contribution to the household.

Thus, on Raroia, children are given regular duties at the age of three, which is very young—even for Polynesia. Samoan children at a slightly older age must run errands, perform household duties, feed chickens, fetch water. In Tahiti, by ten, they, and especially boys, help with the gardens as they doubtless also do in many other parts of Polynesia. Hawaiian children also begin household duties at an early age. The girls are more likely to centre on the indoors—cooking, cleaning and so on—whereas the boys look after the yard and the car. In Tonga boys, though they are not assigned caretaking duties, must help their sisters and do what they ask, for in Tonga sisters have authority. Margaret Mead described the pre-teen years of a Samoan girl as the worst stage in her life. During this time they are 'incessantly at the beck and call of their elders . . . [and] tyrannised over by two-year-old tyrants'(75, p. 30).

Chores are a bind, but they are also explicit, so that once you have done them, you are free of them, at least for the time being. You do not need to think about them. You just do them. Therefore, the additional hidden message in the allocation of chores is the acceptance of that which responsible authority imposes. If you meet these obligations, you are free.

We should note in passing that in our general (non-Maori) child rearing research in New Zealand, hardly any parents expected four-year-old children to be capable of regular chores(97). To expect such was unthinkable. One asks, is there anything serious that a child can contribute to the well-being of a household? They may take out milk bottles, collect the newspaper, maybe go to the shop, but overall these are trivial tasks in no way comparable to helping weed the cassava patch, fish the lagoon or care for a younger child of the family.

Life in Polynesia is not, however, one endless round of chores and looking after children. Both within the home, around the home and away from the home there are lots of times when children make their own entertainments and amusements with each other. In Samoa, Holmes reports:

> Children also find time for play. They play cricket, tag, marbles, and a Samoan variety of hopscotch. They swim, pelt one another with Tahitian chestnuts, fashion toy sail boats out of sardine cans and coconut leaves, or make pull toys out of two tiny immature coconuts connected with a stick (like a bar bell). Playing with dolls, however, is not a Samoan pastime. Perhaps the leisure time activity most enjoyed is group singing and dancing. On moonlight nights (the best time for play) little clusters of children can be found on the village green (*malae*)

singing and clapping in unison while one after another gets up to perform his or her version of the *siva*. When adults hold dances in connection with *malaga* entertainments, the chief spectators are always children who stand outside the house and offer their own imitations of what they observe going on inside(49, p. 79).

Even in a port town like Apia, there are open spaces where children gather, between houses or along the seafront in the evenings; places to laugh and joke and make their own fun, or walk up a stream bed to find a favourite swimming hole. In cultures with a brother–sister avoidance rule, children will play in same-sex groups.

In Rakau we found it hard as outsiders and adults to gain entry to these groups of young children or even find out where they were, though the field worker who dealt with these age groups, Margaret Earle, did as best she could(31). In terms of the nature of the activity, children everywhere probably find much the same occupations, but there are some stylistic differences about children's groups in Polynesia about which, at some risk, we are prepared to generalise.

Firstly, these groups are not characteristically, at least for school age children, led. They do not usually have permanent leaders. There is a consensus leadership. The activities flow rather than switch as a result of decisions. In political terms, they certainly do not have an authority structure, but it is probably inappropriate to call them democratic. The children get caught up in the flow of consensus. They also tend to be inclusive rather than exclusive, a characteristic noted by Ted and Nancy Graves which we will discuss more, as they have done, in the context of schooling(44). In the play group situation the activity scoops up and includes anybody who wishes to join in, covering virtually any preadolescent who can keep up, three to thirteen and beyond.

It is very unusual in Western play groups to find any activity into which children of such a wide age range can join. The Western theory of how children grow is that each age has its nature and its developmental tasks and that to mix ages may lead to conflict or unworkable situations or reduce enjoyment. Not only is each child an individual but each age is separate, and almost every child activity is age graded—often sex divided too. And mostly children stay close to home and adult supervision.

In Polynesia when children are free of chores and obligations around the home they go out into the wider environment. To stay close to home might lead to adult scrutiny and disapproval or to more chores. Freedom is better enjoyed elsewhere. And elsewhere is everywhere.

Solidarity is important, for without it the peer group would fail to give the emotional support and security which is one of its prime psychological functions. It is not so much solidarity against the adult or parental world but simply solidarity apart from it. But solidarity often means ensuring that adults will not interfere—and this sometimes means subterfuge. Here is a quote from the modern Hawaiian situation that could be echoed in Samoa, the Cook Islands or New Zealand or anywhere in Polynesia. There are tactics involved; it is as well to learn them well and early too:

> Rather than negotiation with adults, which is rarely possible, young people often share the work and resolve problems among themselves, reducing the need for adult leadership and intervention in order to accommodate personal interests, needs and plans.

One senior girl who was the eldest sister gave an explicit description (reported in Field Notes) of these tactics: She asked to be in an evening activity at school and her father refused her permission because the mother worked at night and he needed her at home. She surmised that he didn't want to be bothered by the younger children. The first evening she volunteered to do the dishes for her next oldest sister if she would babysit the kids. After cleaning up the kitchen she asked her father for a ride, and mentioned the sister would take care of the 'small kids'. He had just seen the girl doing the dishes. She got to go. On later evenings she brought the siblings snacks and provided the helpful sister with a running account of events and tickets to the eventual performance. Apparently her father was content for the eldest to participate and even to provide her a ride as long as the tasks were taken care of, even though he had originally refused her request. The initiative in figuring out satisfactory conditions was up to her and the negotiation was with siblings rather than him. His input was not to care who did what in the solution. The younger sister had had some hopes to be in the activity, but relief from her disliked dishwashing and a chance to hear what was going on and see the performance was certainly better than the turndown her father would have given a request to go. Our informant concluded with the comment, 'We take turns that way', indicating a chance to go out gained by cooperation would go to the sister another time. It became evident that parents were content to have tasks performed in any way a group of siblings could work out(38, pp. 148-149).

After all, so long as parental demands are met and no interference is created with the world of adult concerns, adults are simply not very interested in what children are doing. Certainly, if a child finds it hard to get on with the gang, or feels victimised, there is little point in seeking adult intervention and the child who tells tales may even be prevented from doing so. Children of this age are supposed to work it out with other children and in this way they are consolidating the Polynesian pattern of cooperative group solidarity and problem solving by consensus. Getting along together becomes very important for children and as they learn to do it they can turn to one another for mutual protection and defence. Thus cooperation maximises freedom. Unreasonable parents are likely to find that the child's response is to become devious.

A parent or adult who is wise, in the Polynesian sense and setting, recognises that children will get their own way because the alternative is the exercise of a parental vigilance that is simply not part of the parenting prescription in Polynesia, whether applied by adults or caretakers. In Polynesia, the knack of achieving adult control over children, and there are times when this is necessary, is through other children.

What are the negative effects of peer socialisation? Though among themselves children may chatter volubly we wonder about the quality of the language used. There is obviously a different kind of goal setting and goal attainment when children, not adults, call the tune. What happens to achievement motivation which, so the psychological literature says, develops by careful and even gradients of attainment at or about the eighth year? Do groups inflict conformity? Do peers tolerate, value, appreciate, promote diversity? What of the cruelty of which children are as capable as any other human beings? What of the loneliness of those who feel excluded?

We do not know about these things. We have clear indications that given the chance some quite young children will leave home, either in village or town, and run away to live. In his Fijian study *My Friends the Shoeshine Boys* Dennis Oliver tells of these eight, nine, ten-year-old boys, waifs on the streets of Suva, and how they responded to his programme of training(85). The patterns of peer association are there but what the boys learn in the city is a sort of survival rather than socialisation to a culture. Much the same could be said for the suburban Maori children in Auckland, New Zealand, who spend all night at disco dances in the centre of the town. They *can't* go home because the buses stop running but they *don't* go home earlier because they are happy to be with their peers. Is this a desirable form of modern Polynesian childhood?

Though we will discuss formal education in school in detail later, we cannot leave the world of children without mentioning what a serious intrusion formal schooling has been and will continue to be in the Polynesian system of socialisation. As Margaret Mead stated: 'This brings about a complete disorganization of the . . . households, which have no precedents for a manner of life where mothers have to stay at home and take care of their children and adults have to perform small routine tasks and run errands'(75, p. 30).

School takes away the caretakers for a large part of the day. Children's chores now have to be confined to either the early morning or the end of the day. The formal organisation of the school takes little account of the style of peer group activities, depending largely on a culturally foreign pattern of adult directed learning and individual pursuit of excellence. There is probably no Western institution whose effect has been as disruptive of the Polynesian socialisation pattern as the school. Were children given the choice, they would probably never go to school at all. The power and the potency belong with the people and the pattern. It is the community and the peer experience that appeal, set the style and provide the satisfaction as children grow. Against this, the school may be seen to offer very little except that it is where the peers are! That is why Polynesian children go to school.

The pattern of peer socialisation will persist in spite of schooling, social change and urbanisation. Because it is so different from Western adult directed and controlled socialisation it is not always given the recognition or support needed or is regarded as neglect or an infringement of some right of children to be protected from each other! Perhaps what children everywhere need is what Polynesian children can so easily enjoy—a world of their own.

CHAPTER 7

Achievement—With a Little Help From my Friends

'When I look at Fijian educational achievement I begin to think that maybe there is something lacking or rather not enough pressures from Fijian parents in socialising their children towards high level goals.'

'The Fijians' rather rigid social political structure together with their Christian world view suppresses the hope for achievement and the motivation needed for educational and economic achievement. As I see it, the notion of the life after death and the lesser importance of this life compared to the spiritual after-life might be a very influential factor in the consideration of the rural Fijian level of achievement. When you are constantly being reminded by parents, teachers, ministers and close relatives that what is important is the preparation for the after-life and that the utmost reward man can achieve is to reach the Kingdom of God, this, together with a social structure with its pressures, obligations and real or imaginary social sanctions creates a psychological barrier in which the rural Fijian finds himself entangled.'

'The desire for formal education has changed some aspects of the Samoan perception of achievement. Competitiveness is now found in villages as it adds to the status and prestige of parents. I can still, however, sense the feeling or the meaning of achievement in the old days in the way that one had to be a good provider not only for his family but also for the community. It could also mean being a good speaker, orator, kind and benevolent if a matai.'

'I have just realised that the intention of having four different "houses" in my former boarding school was a way of introducing a system of competing within a setting of cooperation. The girls were divided into four houses and there was competition between them in sports, dormitory cleanliness, personal tidiness etc., for the "best house" trophy towards the end of the year. It was a very effective way of getting the girls to work together as a community and also to compete with the other houses.'

At a finer level of analysis we might continue to extract more particular, less general, patterns from the literature of childhood in the cultures of Polynesia. But the five strands we have drawn out, the importance of community, multiple parenting, early indulgence, early independence and peer socialisation are by far the most obvious and generally agreed. We shall now turn, in the remaining chapters, to see how these factors affect some major aspects of psychological functioning in Polynesian development.

During the decade of the sixties, a number of research workers in varying locations around the Pacific became interested in the way in which achievement is patterned in different parts of Polynesia(3, 38, 91, 107). Their approaches, while they shared a common background of psychological theory, were at first so varied that it was difficult to separate differences in cultural patterning from the particular biases and orientations of those reporting it. Furthermore, because this problem presented itself largely as an educational one, a large part of the reason for their interest derived from conflicts that arise in fitting Polynesian character into the Western institution of the school.

Sometimes this led to over-simplification, as in our own earlier Rakau studies where a lack of school success was taken to indicate an absence of the motivation to achieve(91). The standard method of measuring the need for achievement, developed by David McClelland, consists of four pictures about which people are asked to make up stories(66). When in these stories an individual mentions success, that scores a plus, failure a minus. The method is supposed to measure how much a person has fantasies about achievement and *that* is supposed to measure how strong their achievement motivation may be. Consistently, the use of McClelland's technique has shown very little difference between such widely differing groups as Ausubel's urban and rural samples of Maori children, or Gallimore and his associates' samples of Hawaiians who do well at high school and those who do not(3, 38). On this fantasy task all these groups have about the same level of day dreaming about success. But they do not all succeed equally well nor do they display any great preoccupation with getting ahead in real life. Polynesian children have no difficulty in responding to demands for achievement provided that they are not forced into conflict between their desire to raise their own status and their need to be part of a group(107). Thus we will present our discussion in terms of these two linked patterns of motivation: affiliation and achievement.

We need to go back a little to look at the basic theory of the development of achievement motivation which McClelland developed through many years of study. This assumes that in the course of early childhood, children have developed in them a need to achieve, to a greater or lesser extent, as a result of the ways in which parents reward or do not reward achieving behaviour. High levels result from careful goal setting by parents in graduated steps up to or about the age of eight. McClelland, however, considers that the level of an individual's need to achieve can be raised by appropriate training at any stage of life and he has demonstrated that this can be done.

However, the theory has been developed within a Western context and contains Western biases. For one thing, the idea that behaviour springs from inside an individual is heavily linked to Western ideas of ideal character structure. What is desirable achieving behaviour in America may be regarded as excessive immoral egoism in Japan(29). Indeed, modern personality theory has moved away from the idea of a measurable personality structure inside the person towards a much more realistic, complicated and sophisticated view of the person as responding to characteristic situations in which the individual recognises certain possibilities and moves towards them(79). A person is motivated by chances 'out there' rather than by tendencies inside him or her. But to us both sources of motivation would seem important and undoubtedly are.

It is simply untrue (and rather silly) to state that Polynesians are not achievers or that they merely fail to be motivated by opportunities. They are searching for success in ways that Westerners do not recognise as achievement. Their achievement satisfactions are gained in cultural contexts. When you use a fantasy measure of need for achievement the method of measurement becomes the situation. Perhaps for Polynesians the stimulus is very standardised and because it is standard you get standard results. With nothing to gain, and nothing to lose, Polynesian children will give compliant stereotyped answers, particularly where, as almost everywhere, they have developed quite sophisticated techniques of dealing with intrusive people from 'the other culture'.

Now let us turn to some particular writings on this matter. In Rakau the things that mattered in adult life were the maintenance of the community boundaries that allowed people inside to identify themselves as Maori, to maintain a pattern of participation in the shifting changing nature of social and family politics, to avoid being isolated from the community by the community and to maintain one's place in the diffuse pattern of social obligation(91). Though we said then that achievement was negatively sanctioned, a more precise formulation would be that achievement could only be gained through the group. A wealthy and successful individual paid his social depts along the way and would be as concerned for the general welfare as for that of his own self or that of his family.

The Hawaiian material explores the matter in great depth but the conclusion is consistent: a group of high achieving boys (i.e. boys who were doing well at school) had no higher achievement motivation than a group of boys who were not succeeding in school(38, 52). However, boys and girls who scored high on need affiliation (directing activity towards human relationship goals) also scored high on a measure of school success (reading achievement)(108).

This is a new idea that fills out the picture. Whereas Westerners are motivated by the need to achieve in terms of material success and social advancement, Polynesians are motivated by a need to please others, to keep up patterns of social ease in relationships, to get others to act warmly towards them.

Because of the emphasis in the community in which Gallimore and Howard worked on interdependence, young people there can be motivated to achieve provided that the situation allows them to work in terms of group goals: 'To capitalize on the social proclivities of the students, we abandoned the idea of trying to break up conversations; instead, we tried to channel peer interactions by forming teams whose members were directed toward a mutually meaningful goal'(69, p. 104).

What early independence and peer socialisation add up to is not rugged individualism but a sensitivity to social interdependence against which an individual will not move, from which he or she has no wish to be separated.

Levy does not discuss achievement as a technical matter, but when he speaks of Tahitian feelings and particularly the restraint on unfriendly hostile and aggressive actions he provides information on the same need to temper personal expression in terms of the group(61). It's all right to be ashamed or timid or sad in Tahiti and fine to be happy and friendly and loving, to be moved by the social spirit of things and when one is not, one either changes the task or has a rest, leaves the situation, or just turns off. The great goal of social training in Tahiti is to integrate people into social systems.

Margaret Mead discussed the avenues open for achievement for a young Samoan village based youth:

> There are several types of activities in one of which he must specialize. He must become a house-builder, a fisherman, an orator, or a wood-carver. Proficiency in some technique must set him off a little from his fellows . . . And with this goes the continual demand that he should not be too efficient, too outstanding, too precocious. He must never exceed his fellows by more than a little. He must arouse neither their hatred nor the disapproval of his elders, who are far readier to encourage and excuse the laggard than to condone precocity(75, p. 35).

Such motivational patterns are, of course, exactly what one would expect from a diffuse caretaking system which develops great social sensitivities. Since the initial warmth of early experience was distributed so that one received early pleasure and satisfaction from a great many people, why should one run the risk or pay the price of isolating oneself from the continued enjoyment of social supports? Personal bonding between parent and child, which has recently become so emphasised in the literature of child development, is dramatically opposed to the Polynesian conception of distributed emotional support and truly social security. Why put all your emotional eggs in one basket? Why strive for individual excellence when all you will get for it is criticism and scorn?

There is one Polynesian culture, for which there is information, where the balance is different and that is Rotuma(51). There the training of children remains a matter of direct parental attention. Rotuman parents maintain a dominant concern for minimising social conflict. They want their children to be good citizens of Rotuman society and they educate them accordingly. Howard says that they so act towards their children that the child incurs an enormous social debt which parents use to control and influence their behaviour. They rarely punish except when children wander away from home without permission and their behaviour is corrected with good humour and warmth. Parents, of course, in this context means adults, not just the biological parents. Howard specifically mentions that children are encouraged with subtle praise, non-verbal approval and are told to attend to adult models, to watch a skilful adult in action. Rotumans develop a characteristic Polynesian social sensitivity but through the use of more adult guidance than elsewhere. Undoubtedly some degree of sibling caretaking must occur, but throughout Howard's account his emphasis is on direct training by adults of children in a climate of cooperation, social warmth and restraint. It would also seem that there is no break in the indulgent attitudes which surround childhood so that it is not until children go to school that they are subject to any other than the supporting influence that they have come to expect from their parents.

Under these circumstances the development of individual achievement appears to be higher. Howard states that Rotuman children are very keen competitors. However, the Polynesian obligation to act in social terms is still extremely strong and it would also seem likely that, on this small island with only seven schools, the school system has adapted more compatibly to the affiliative demands of Polynesian culture. Howard gives examples of group work methods being used. In Rotuma, where adults have been the important socialisers, the role of the teacher, he thinks, presents no conflict to the children. They transfer to his or her model.

Howard reports that a teacher would reward a child by allowing him or her to work independently. That just wouldn't work for Polynesians anywhere else because to work alone has very little satisfaction.

In the Rotuman home setting, parents and adults are intensely interested in their children's success at school. When they do well parents will encourage them to study and increase the pressures towards school success. But if they do not do well at school, they are not rejected; the children are encouraged to do subsistence tasks instead of homework, and will be praised for their efforts in this direction. They will become the Rotumans who continue to live on the island; the others may well decide to depart. It seems that the Rotumans allocate success to the successful. Howard reports that at all levels of the school system it is easy to discriminate between the achievers and the non-achievers. This is a pattern that has developed on an island which has always had a large out-migration but whose people wanted their migrants to do well.

We can sum up by saying that everywhere in Polynesia, Rotuma included, the development of achievement stands in marked contrast to the intensity of socialisation which is typical of the Western family where the emphasis is so strong that the development of personal achievement is unquestioned, a cultural given. Well, we question the Western way; and so, we feel, would most

Polynesians. Modern Polynesians should ask themselves most carefully whether there is any need to incorporate Western influence of this kind. Their societies, after all, can well continue to be places where status is not entirely determined by personal achievement and effort. Though they have become open societies to a greater degree than was traditionally the case, they do not need to be wide open to the disturbing excesses of Western individualism with its attendant anxieties and exploitations.

Thomas has conducted a number of experiments to explore cooperation and competition among children in various Polynesian settings(109, 110). He uses various research tasks in which children may employ cooperative, rivalrous (competitive) or individualistic (self-seeking) strategies. He recognises that in most Polynesian settings rivalry between groups may be quite intense, as when Maoris play rugby league or Samoans cricket, or in dance or other cultural competitions. But only in urban areas, or islands heavily influenced by Western development, does one find individualistic and competitive behaviour.

He speaks of such children and Western children as having a 'cooperation deficit' such that they are unable to cooperate even when cooperation is the most appropriate behaviour. He advises teachers of Polynesian children to use teaching strategies that maximise cooperation and interdependent group learning.

Since parents and adults are not involved in this pattern of peer cooperation their influence on children continues to be somewhat authoritarian. Respect is so important that it is proper to expect authority to be recognised. What effect does this have on achievement?

There is little research evidence on this. Thomas reports that teachers urge children to stand on their own feet and try to encourage individual excellence, and no doubt pastors and parents do too. But in the long run they are not the ones the children live with. The voice of authority does matter to the children. They listen with respect (mostly). But the injunction is not very functional; the costs are too high. The urging creates for them a problem—it does not solve it.

In some ways this situation parallels the phenomenon that Martina Horner has called fear of success(50). She, speaking of women, believes that when a woman is faced with the choice of being successful or remaining within the stereotype of being feminine, social forces push her towards giving up her desire for academic or vocational success. Such women may still be successful wives and mothers but if they become career women it seems to them that it may be at the expense of being feminine.

Are Polynesians caught in a similar kind of trap? Is there always a conflict when they need to go it alone? Not if they are succeeding for their group, their tribe, their island, their village, their church, their football team and so on. So long as they have secure roots of identity in a group when they succeed there will be 'home' people who will be proud of them and they will not be running the risk of alienating themselves from their community.

CHAPTER 8

Gaining Status: Giving Respect

> 'In Samoa one knows not only one's place but also the obligation to other members of the community or the extended family and what is expected from them. Within this setting, there is always room to manoeuvre. A person can earn more or promote to a high status, or reclaim a title that had been lost if his obligation is well performed. His personal qualities and his properties also contribute to his status.'
>
> 'Education is now seen as an appropriate means for upward mobility apart from our traditional mode of promotion [in Tonga]. I myself was born as an ordinary commoner. But when I finish here, I will assume a socioeconomic status higher and more important than my former classmates and colleagues.'

The development of intricate status systems is one of the major hallmarks of Polynesian cultures. Years ago the anthropologist Ruth Benedict, seeking to simplify all the detail of what a people do, introduced the idea of culture as a pattern of behaviour formed around particular focal ideas(11). Thus among the Kwakiutl of the Canadian north-west coast the ceremonies termed potlatch identify a preoccupation with competitive acquisition, display and destruction of personal property as a central pattern. By studying potlatch ceremonies the whole complicated system of Kwakiutl status, wealth, ownership and competitiveness is revealed. Every culture, in a similar way, generates a particular set of human problems for which its folkways then provide a solution.

In Polynesia there are many subsidiary patterns of this kind, as, for example, between when it is right to act cooperatively and when competitively but it seems to us, and to most people who have looked at Polynesian cultures, that Goldman was right when he identified the central preoccupation of Polynesia as one of status and of rivalry between people of similar or different statuses(42, 43).

This preoccupation appears in different ways. In Maori society

Gaining Status: Giving Respect   81

you can subtly introduce references to one's ancestry into one's oratory. Thus you not only establish who you are but also recognise the status of others around you. The criterion is primarily genealogical; to be a firstborn son of a line of firstborn sons gives paramount status. But as Metge points out, there are at least four terms that relate to status; *kaumatua* (elder, spokesman), *rangatira* (aristocrat), *ariki* (chief) and *tohunga* (expert)(77). There are actually more; for women the term *kuia* is a term used for any female who has begun to act ceremonially in the *marae* situation; she is no longer a *hine* or a *wahine*, the more ordinary terms for women. The male equivalent is *koro*, old man of status. The terms *teina* (younger brother of a boy or younger sister of a girl), *tuakana* (older brother of a boy), *tungane* (brother of a girl) and *tuahine* (sister), *tupuna* (elder) and *mokopuna* (loosely—grandchild) may all be used to refer to unchangeable status relationships. Most Polynesian forms of addressing relatives recognise gender, older and younger and generation in similar ways.

The status with which one is born is not, however, entirely fixed, because in relation to any other person around one it can be manipulated by careful location within the widespread and complicated network of a bilateral kinship system. In such a system both lines of descent, from mother's and father's clans, can be made active. Since both mother and father had both a mother and father you can quickly activate an enormous spread of kinship information. You can also call upon the ancestor that you wish to, for the purposes of the moment, to establish precedence over another individual who is, of course, doing the same in rivalry. So even in genealogical terms, before ever one draws on personal attributes or successes, this cultural status game can become very subtle, very complex and the dexterous use of kinship information a much admired cultural skill. The whole network is constantly changing as people die or leave the area. Older men and women who know the rules will enjoy the mock battles involved immensely. But you lose status by being too blatant. The essence is to reveal, but not to exhibit.

But things become more complicated still because, whatever one's genealogical standing may be, it is raised or lowered by one's personal history of accomplishment and by the way one is handling any situation at the moment. This is one aspect of what is termed *mana* and you will find it is important everywhere in Polynesia. The attainment of *mana* is made more tricky because one must not be seen to seek it. The cultural rule, throughout Polynesia, is that though others recognise *mana* in a person, self-seeking for its attainment almost guarantees that it will not be granted. The higher one's status the more humble one should appear to be; conversely, when a Polynesian expresses humility it may be in the expectation that his or her status will be recognised.

In social terms status allocates precedence, rights, duties and obligations and is reflected in every aspect of life. A Polynesian knows who the head of his or her family may be. Similarly, the important people in a community are known to everybody and can, if necessary, be ranked. A formal occasion such as a wedding or a funeral or greetings to an important visitor will call forth the mechanisms of status so that they are clearly seen in, for example, the order of precedence in serving the ceremonial liquor in a Samoan *kava* ceremony or in Maori oratory.

Traditionally, the status of the *ariki* in the Maori case, the *ali'i* in Hawaii, the *matai* in Samoa, the *ari'i* in Tahiti, the *aliki* on Pukapuka or the *nopeli* (noble families of Tonga) carried a common set of expectations. The chief was not often called upon to display chieftainship publicly; men spoke for him or her. The chiefly obligation was to serve the people, silently, indirectly, through others as agent. Though through the power of the office great feasts could be called, often the chief lived in comparative (sometimes abysmal) poverty, dispensing and dispersing the collective wealth to level undue accumulation and to see that sharing was equal. The chief had power and authority in matters of dispute, especially those affecting the corporate assets such as land or in resolving other status conflicts as in marriage. These days much of this may have faded. In Fiji, our students told us, chiefs are now likely to be personally very wealthy.

It has become a commonplace of Pacific anthropology that Polynesian cultures have hereditary chieftainship and Melanesian do not. It is a sweeping generalisation but it contains a germ of truth, because in the Solomons or in a Papua New Guinea village acknowledgment of headman status is all that is needed. In Polynesia that is not enough. Ability in an able person will be recognised but when a chief dies no successor would be appointed on that basis alone.

Yet inheritance of status is not always down through the line of first sons, not always to males only. When a chief dies a new chief must be found: succession is not automatic. In some New Zealand tribes and in Fiji (at least in the Western Division tribes) the status of chieftain-maker is a separate status held and inherited in a particular family, usually in another tribe. This useful device puts the choice of a new leader outside the immediate kin group, just as the British Queen stands outside parliament yet calls on a person within to form a government. It reduces conflict, cuts through rivalry over status.

Whereas in most of Polynesia the primary signifiers of rank were genealogical and the intensity of cultural awareness extended back in time, some observers, especially Mead, have emphasised that for Samoa things are different(76). She says, 'The interest in a shared and immutable version of the past has been modified by the use of titles rather than names and the preoccupation with the construction of local hierarchies by the manipulation of the relative rank of the titles' (p. 127).

In Samoa, families, villages, districts and regions are part of an assumed system in which every title is given a place. But this is not fixed and Mead says there is a fair amount of local autonomy in rearranging the system. Furthermore, one receives a title by election and one will only be elected when one has carefully paid one's dues to family and village obligations. In Maori, there is a term for doing so—*whakaiti*—the obligation to be humble; the higher the status, the greater the obligation. Samoans, too, display status by humility of expression. By putting yourself down, you put yourself up. But the process is tricky. A *matai* of our acquaintance said, 'If a *matai* lowers himself to an extent that is degrading to the extended family, then his family will tell him, in no uncertain terms, that this has been the case.'

Everywhere in Polynesia an individual grows up so immersed in the status system and its dynamics that he or she may scarcely be aware of the fact. Furthermore, since it is a low status thing to display status, children must learn from a very early age when a high status person is just grandfather round the house and will give the child cuddles and attention and when he is so engaged in the duties of status that he will not. We have often seen a grandchild run onto the *marae* (ceremonial meeting ground) while an orator is speaking, clutch at his legs and be totally ignored. While there have been studies of such things as the communication system of status elites and of the kinship basis of status in various Polynesian cultures, there are no studies of how children learn to recognise the complex and diffuse indicators of status in Polynesian cultures(57). Mead wrote that children in Samoa:

... must learn to sit or crawl within the house and never to stand upright unless it is absolutely necessary; never to address an adult in a standing position; to stay out of the sun; not to tangle the strands of a weaver; not to scatter the cut-up coconut which is spread out to dry; to keep their scant loin cloths at least nominally fastened to their persons; to treat fire and knives with proper caution; not to touch the *kava* bowl or the *kava* cup; and if their father is a chief, not to crawl on his bed-place when he is by(75, p. 26).

And one of our students from Samoa said:

About children learning about status-gaining and qualities pertaining to status—they have all the opportunity to observe this at an early age. If they do not, they are forced to by the disciplinary treatment they receive like not walking through the house when there are visitors present. If asked to enter the house, they do so in a crouch saying '*tulou*' or seating themselves before speaking. In other words, the adults provide incidental traditional education in these matters thereby exposing the children right through youth to who is important. Their reactions to people of high status are carefully guided and they are trained to be respectful at all times. This I think is the most important point which is often missed by writers; that the upbringing of the Samoan (if not Polynesian) child is a guided one throughout, interspersed with severe lessons on status gaining and observance of certain societal conventions. It is usually the women-folk who give this part of traditional education by their incidental remarks—the fathers comment on this and at times reprimand when they see fit to do so. The latter part of the training is done by fathers. Thus from infancy to adolescence, the Samoan youngster is continually reminded of status by 'lessons' he observes and incidental ones when severely reprimanded.

Mead summarises: 'These are really simply a series of avoidances, enforced by occasional cuffings and a deal of exasperated shouting and ineffectual conversation'(75, p. 26).

The emphasis in reports about the New Zealand Maori and modern Hawaiians on how children learn to read social cues is relevant. From this we can generalise that in the peer group children learn to read the social indications of the state of those around them within the group and of those adults around them upon whose actions the freedom and autonomy of the peer group depends. And status recognition, information and respect requirements spread from child to child within the peer group.

In every Polynesian society children, so long as they do not interfere, may be participant observers in most aspects of family, village, informal or ceremonial life—children may even be present at a birth and certainly are aware of the ceremonies around death. In Samoa children are not allowed near the body if the dead person is of high rank and in Tonga it depends on the degree of relationship to the dead person. They may passively observe the rituals of gift giving on almost any important occasion and even the precedents recognised in the serving of *kava*, though nowhere are children allowed to participate in such ceremonies. Thus there are any number of opportunities for them to observe the nature of the status system and the rules by which the game is played. Our problem, as psychologists, is to explain how all this incidental information is incorporated by the growing child so that they come to know their way around in this complex and changing maze of social relationships and what system of rewards and punishments maintains this behaviour.

Does the expectation that they may someday have to participate play some part in their learning? Does the fact that their own families, to whom presumably they are emotionally attached, are involved focus their attention and facilitate learning? Punishment for transgression of the formal rules of status recognition clearly has a role. Children will certainly be aware that for adults status matters are a continual part of the social commentary of gossip, a way of providing feedback to the actors in the drama of social status. One of the great differences between peer groups in Polynesia and elsewhere is that while they operate apart from adult scrutiny, what is going on in the adult world is always a matter of concern. The adults may or may not be watching the children but the children are certainly watching the adults, if for no other reason than to know when to get out of their way or when to dodge a flying fist. Something on which adults place as much importance as status is bound to seem important to growing children even though they themselves are not ranked. One day, when they become part of the adult world, they will have to operate on these terms so they had best learn how to avoid punishing consequences before it happens.

Anyone concerned with Polynesia in any way must recognise how very different this concept of status is from what is usually referred to in social science literature as socioeconomic status. Social scientists simply do not seem to realise how ethnocentric the latter concept is. More widely than this, Europeans quite frequently make the assumption that, because some Polynesians do not seem to be very interested in acquiring status by Western criteria of wealth, material goods and property or education, they are not interested in status at all. So important is status in Polynesia that to come to this conclusion is to miss entirely what has held Polynesian cultures together and given them shape and form in changing circumstances.

In later chapters we will consider how the perpetuation of Polynesian status systems continues in changing and modern circumstances and how introduced and rather intrusive systems such as Western education have created difficulties and problems.

It has been our purpose in this chapter simply to indicate that in various ways status is alive and well and living in Polynesia. There are developmental processes which link sibling rivalry and the family, getting on with one another in the peer group and the balancing of status rivalry in the adult community. We can do no more than indicate here that this is an important topic for further research. We suspect that complex social structures are more likely to have associated with them multiple caretaking and strong peer socialisation influences. Unfortunately, Weisner and Gallimore did not include variables relating to social structure in their analysis of child and sibling caretaking, its antecedents and its consequences(117).

Westerners looking at adult–child interactions in Polynesian settings are often impressed by what they see as sharp and rather blatant authoritarianism. That is a judgment based on Western values. Polynesia has its authority systems. They are structural and traditional and they do not necessarily imply all that Western psychology reads into the concept of authoritarianism(1). The historical origins are quite different and so are the social and cultural dynamics. For a ramified system of status differences to survive the teaching of respect is, however, an absolute necessity. There is probably no greater shame than inadvertently to be disrespectful. Teaching respect is a parental preoccupation. Giving respect may shut one's mouth and make one seem dumb. The head must hang. The glance be averted. The tone drop. Respect may seem to a Westerner to be shyness, withdrawal, sullenness even, but it is respect, just respect.

One of the prime features of the Polynesian status system, for all that we have said about it, is its fluidity. It may seem, as in Samoa where the precedence of titles is written down, that the system is very rigid indeed, or that in Tonga the fixing by the missionaries of the nobility system has set a flexible system into an iron mould. But in fact, the day to day events of Polynesian life subtly change the relative status of individuals. Were these matters fixed, everyone could accept the situation and no longer be concerned with it. That it is so much a matter of concern clearly indicates that it is a moving and changing world of cultural preoccupation into which one is born. To escape is to cease to be Polynesian.

CHAPTER 9

Coming of Age

> 'During my early upbringing in Fiji I was not encouraged to mix with the opposite sex so while at secondary school I had a hard time mixing around with girls. I did not know how to behave and relate to them and because of this I could not easily associate with female friends. This was made worse by the fact that most of the schools I attended were not co-educational.'
>
> 'Traditionally, in Tonga, girls are assigned to the task of child caring. This practice as I see it helps girls to become isolated and show more individualistic and competitive behaviours.'
>
> 'In my homeland [Tonga] women are more competitive in orientation. They are closely guarded because there is a lot of stress on their virginity. Mothers compete as to who has the best-cared-for daughters. This competitiveness and rivalry between women can grow so great that it will split the whole clan.'

Given the background and context of childhood in Polynesian cultures and the nature of the complexities of adult status, it is obvious that in a traditional setting some transition from childhood to adulthood would be observed. And such was the case, though in different ways in different cultures. Nowadays the recognition of maturity is more likely to occur with less ceremonial marking, though in many locations the rituals of the church have been assimilated into those of the tribe. But it is probably wrong to say that they have replaced them. Certainly in the village situation, such as in Aitutaki, even if a ritual such as supercision (slitting the upper prepuce) is no longer practised it was present twenty or thirty years ago(6). And from Levy's more recent account, the ritual of supercision is still practised in Tahiti(56). In some places, Pukapuka and New Zealand, it has never been reported(7, 14). But supercision is not the important thing. It is merely one of a number of ways in which, for both boys and girls, the transition to adult identity is marked.

Though the presence of definite markers of this transition might make the disturbance of growing up and coming of age less complicated than is the case in Western societies, we would caution against the reading into Polynesian settings of either the sort of generalisations that are made about adolescence in Western text books of psychological development or of simplistic views about its psychological ease. Unlike Western societies, where adult status is given or assigned by adult recognition, it has always been true of Polynesian societies that the transition is made by the decision and the actions of the individual, when he or she indicates. This may be less true in the case of girls, where first menstruation is the chief marker of adult womanhood. But even there it is for the individual to assume the new status, to act accordingly and for the most part joyfully, but also with regrets for childhood now past and misgivings and anxieties about the new status. For both sexes, adulthood is status—that state which adults have and children do not, that state which one has observed for so many years and into which other adults quite comfortably welcome and accept the new heir.

Compared with Melanesia or many parts of Africa the traditional rituals of transition in Polynesian cultures were mild and festive. More than anything else they were welcoming rituals in which previous family status was reaffirmed, sexual maturity recognised and the name to be used thereafter either confirmed or bestowed.

The Polynesian attitude towards names is a characteristic combination of formality and informality. A child at birth or soon after may be named after almost anything at all, as we saw in a previous chapter, but sooner or later the informal name will be replaced by a traditional family or ancestral name.

In New Zealand the process is different; a formal name is decided upon soon after birth, usually by the parents but often in consultation with older members of the family, but the child will be referred to by an informal name (e.g. Buttercup, Raindrops, Boy) and the formal name will be used again, these days when the child enters school. While still by no means common, there is a growing practice among Maoris at or about adulthood to reassert Maori identity by adopting a traditional Maori name, often one given by the highest status person in their family. Clearly, there is a time to be playful about names (and that is childhood) and a time to become serious about them (which is adulthood).

In Niue, in Penryhn and in some other parts of the Cook Islands it is customary for boys to enter manhood by means of a ritual haircut followed by a big church service and a feast. The practice continues, for Penrhyn Islanders at least, in New Zealand. In some parts of the Cooks the first ritual haircut takes place at an earlier age, in Tonga around the fifth birthday. Formal initiation ceremonies usually apply only to males, though on Pukapuka, and perhaps elsewhere, the transition for girls is marked by the adoption of adult dress. Traditionally Polynesian youths presented themselves with their agemates for supercision of the penis. In 1938 the Beagleholes reported that on Tonga busloads of boys in gaily coloured clothes trooped off to the local hospital, where the operation was performed with scissors under local anaesthetic, and then returned home for the feasting(8). Nowadays in Tonga it is done earlier but still with family celebration. But both Holmes and Levy respectively for Samoa and Tahiti report that the operation is done by local practitioners with a razor blade, a bamboo knife or piece of glass(44, 56). In Western Samoa the operation is done shortly after birth. It is interesting to note that where supercision is still done in the village setting, it is accompanied by family or village feasting, but in the case of Tonga, large scale feasting has much declined. Almost everywhere the reason given for the operation is to promote cleanliness but it is also a matter of some shame if it is not performed. In Tahiti, at least, some girls refuse to have intercourse with an unsupercised male. As a rule the requirement of supercision seems matter of fact rather than ceremonious, but where *lavalavas* may slip and some accidental exposure occur one needs to be seen to be proper. Full circumcision, the complete exposure of the glans, is also improper—a man would only unsheath his penis to insult an observer. In Fiji supercision is usually performed around twelve or thirteen years of age and is still an occasion for ceremonial even if done 'Western style' in a hospital. Four nights later it is followed by a feast, as is a girl's first menstruation. Mothers on such occasions feel that complex emotion they call *isa*, a mingling of pride and regret, of joy and sorrow, of love and detachment for a phase passed with all its problems and another begun with all of its.

The real marks of transition are entry to associations of young people, the recognition by adults, though sometimes reluctant, of sexual performance, and participation in the ceremonial life of the family or tribal village, even if only as an apprentice observer.

In Pukapuka, after boys had ceremonially received their adult garb they graduated with further ceremony to the boys' fishing groups and then played a new economic role in the life of the village as more serious providers. In the late 1930s there were separate houses for young men and young women in which those initiated could live if they so chose(7). These were like clubhouses, but most lived at home, and visited the clubhouse from time to time.

In Samoa, a young man ceremoniously seeks the permission of the village council, through his *matai* and with a gift of *kava* root, to enter the *aumaga* or association of untitled men. Permission being granted, he is initiated into the group with his gift of food and by a welcoming speech to which he must reply. He may then take his seat in a position corresponding to the rank of his family head. Teenage girls join the *au'uluma* or unmarried women's association where they serve the village maiden or *taupou*. These days, any woman may be appointed *taupou* for a particular ceremonial occasion as her virtue is no longer in need of protection, and the *aualuma* has become a ceremonial dance group or club that works for civic or church projects(44). These transitions to sex-segregated associations confirm the division of the sexes that has existed for some time but now the peers of a boy or a girl may help arrange liaisons by carrying messages and arranging meetings.

For neither Tahiti, Aitutaki or Tonga are there reports of associations for the young with this degree for formality but the nature of adolescent association groups among the Maori and in Hawaii suggest that though the formal traditional structures have changed, young people support one another in making the transition to adult status through groups that look like gangs in the modern sense (complete with monogrammed jackets, motor cycles and chain epaulettes) but which Metge, speaking for the Maori, regards as a modern equivalent of a traditional function(71). Certainly, in the groups which organise for concert activity and community, service in New Zealand and Hawaii, we see a regeneration in modern adaptive form of the traditional associations of those assuming young adulthood. Here there is a strong revitalisation of interest in such clubs and societies where modern and traditional song, chant, speech making and the use of traditional local language is emphasised. In our view such culture groups certainly are modern regenerations of traditional youth associations; of motor cycle gangs we are not so sure. Their cultural homeland may well be east of the Californian coastline, not west. It all depends on why they do what they do. Any gang cares for its members' welfare. To be Polynesian it must somehow relate to the status and respect system of the adult community its members will some day join.

In sexual affairs, two double standards apply almost everywhere in Polynesia. Firstly, from an adult point of view, and certainly in the eyes of the church, sexual experimentation is not supposed to occur. But it does, and is generally ignored unless the girl becomes pregnant or the parents do not like the partner or the liaison cuts across established status lines. The second double standard allows, in Beaglehole's phrase 'the boy to sow a largish crop of wild oats'(6). Malo makes the same observation about Rotuman practice(66). But in spite of this, young people in the Pacific find sexual relations as interesting, exciting and satisfying as young people anywhere. So Beaglehole reports for Aitutaki and Mead and Holmes for Samoa(6, 44, 69). In Tahiti, things are a little more complicated, and it takes a while for young people to become comfortable with their sexual desires and performances in a society where shame is an important sanction and privacy unlikely(56).

It is worth noting in passing that in Tahiti, among the New Zealand Maori, in Ra'ivavae and possibly in other parts of Polynesia it is not uncommon for a number of young men to have intercourse with one available female, usually the village prostitute, on the same occasion(56, 67). Nowadays this may be considered a crime but it is likely it was quite common in traditional times in some locations—but not in either Tonga or Samoa, where our informants categorically deny its occurrence.

Adult sexual status, then, seems rather easily achieved in most Polynesian societies. To be sexually active is of little account provided pregnancy can be avoided.

The entry into an active role in the ceremonial and festive life of Polynesian communities involves young people more in serving than in participation. For example, they may be involved in the preparation of *kava* in Samoa and Tonga, or working in the cookhouse at a Maori *hui*. In Samoa, however, quite young men may acquire a title and the acquisition and display of the full body tattoo of young Samoan men is a prideful part of their new status. Yound adults, however, are really serving an apprenticeship on ceremonial occasions, which in the case of the Maori male will persist until his father, who always has ceremonial precedence, has died.

Both in New Zealand and in Hawaii, young adults, male and female, are making active efforts through seminars and other forms of study group to recapture the knowledge and skills which will enable them to participate in ceremonial life and perpetuate their own cultural tradition. This may not yet seem necessary in some parts of Polynesia such as Samoa or Tonga, but in the Cooks and in Tahiti dance festivals and competitions provide a clear way in which the cultural identity of young people may be expressed and in so doing they gain great social approval.

To an ever-increasing degree young people in Polynesia are turning to other more European forms of expressing their identity, as in creative writing and the visual arts. Far from declining, the opportunities for young people to express an ethnic identity are undoubtedly growing and will continue to increase.

But ethnic identity and the recognition of adulthood within the village setting are not the whole story, for Western influences are strong, particularly in the economy and in education, and have created new ways in which young people may express personal identity. This may be disturbing both to themselves and to those around them. In Samoa educational success, particularly at a tertiary institution, and a place in the prevailing money economy may lead to a title earlier than if one stayed behind in the village and served the community in the traditional way. But Samoans will work this out in time.

Similarly, the Polynesian groups now permanently settled in Auckland, Honolulu, San Francisco, San Jose, San Mateo and Los Angeles are refashioning community associations through which young people can assume a valid identity in cultural terms. They form church groups, they set up community citizen advice networks, work collectively, and in particular often seek to contribute to their families back on the islands from their increased earnings overseas. For Polynesians, the major factors in the assumption of identity at adolescence lie not in identifying with the idea of adolescence itself but with the rapid transition to adult status. Nevertheless, there was a clear intermediate status, after puberty and before marriage, more that of a young adult than of a person outgrowing childhood. That everywhere Polynesian educational systems have adopted the idea of high schools, which almost demand the imposition of the Western concept of adolescent immaturity, is a powerful source of conflict and problems.

These are created by the high school, not by the Polynesian cultures, and their reformulation in Polynesian terms is a matter of some urgency. Traditional Polynesian cultures had a clear concept of, and a place for, adolescence but as apprentice adults rather than in some hazy interregnum between statuses. The expectations around young adults are not confused. Nevertheless, where the yoke of adult authority, status and respect rides hard, for particular individuals in particular places, this stage can be a private hell. Though no research has been done we have heard reports of adolescent suicide that are quite alarming. When Wendt graphically portrays the stormy passage of an aging *matai* who no longer wants such status he paints an age-reversal of what a young person might go through in gaining it(108). There are possible troubles and torments that lie in wait for any young person in any culture. Though the manufacture of youth culture has largely been a function of Western industrialised society and the education system that it devised to handle industrial employment in complex urban living, and though in that sense that kind of adolescence was and is foreign to Polynesia, unneeded and unwelcome, most Polynesian societies do now need to think constructively about how young people may gain entry to their cultural heritage.

It is unlikely that schools, especially in multi-ethnic situations, can or can be persuaded to do the job. Coming of age in a new time needs new markers, new recognitions so that young people can, with confidence, create their own new forms of old ways.

CHAPTER 10

Her World and His

'When some fishermen returned without any bonito, we used to tease them by saying that it was a team of women that had gone fishing.'

'In Tonga, men appear to be the directors and managers on such occasions as a funeral, a wedding, a fono (village meeting), but behind the scene women are always there with overwhelming influence on the process of decision making.'

'If I were to borrow anything from a neighbour, in Tonga, it is more respectful and safer to ask the women. Why? It is because a man is inclined to be easy-going, whereas women may be sometimes serious and difficult. Because of this, it is felt that when the wife says yes, the husband's bound to say yes, too.'

'I was at a student meeting once when a young man stood up and said "the women in my culture exist to serve the men". You should have heard the roar of disagreement from all the women present.'

'I feel that because God created Adam first and then made Eve out of his rib that we women are supposed to be followers, not leaders.'

'I know a home economics adviser working for the Department of Agriculture. She finds that her job is very difficult because most of the men in the villages she visits do not want to listen to a woman.'

In a group of cultures where the pattern of socialisation is diffused between many caretakers and where the acquisition and maintenance of status is important, one might expect very high levels of anxiety and insecurity. Yet from the earliest research reports right on through until the present, outside observers have commented on the relative absence of both. Therefore, Polynesian cultures must be providing ways in which individuals are taught to cope with difficulties of this sort. One method that eliminates a whole range of possible insecurities is the maintenance of very clear prescriptions for being male and for being female.

Throughout Polynesia, in every culture, you will encounter strong positive mature women whose calming and directing presence provides the anchor point for not only the emotional aspects of family and community living, but for much of the internal day to day political activity. Outsiders may sometimes find some of them rather formidable(59). While it is left to men to become involved in the external public display of conflicts and their resolution, women in a quiet internal way are modulating and managing the same matters, only occasionally stepping into the direct glare of the public area. The women know full well what the display of male status behaviour is about and they take as much notice of it as it deserves; no less and certainly no more. Thus the male and female roles are mirror images of each other in spite of male speaking rights and male primogeniture (descent through the firstborn son). The roles are certainly complementary but they are not equal.

Traditionally, there is good evidence that the formal status position of women is clearly lower than that of men, even if in informal systems they can work to have things their own way. Where infanticide was practised, female children were more likely to be killed than male(34, 61). The public celebration of life events such as initiation is likely to be stressed more for males and in some of the cultures is completely absent for females. While no means universally present, menstrual taboos and restrictions indicate that women were periodically and ritually unclean. Once married they may be almost perpetually pregnant or just recovering from pregnancy for decades of their lives. We have already mentioned that young males were granted greater sexual licence than young women (even though they have to have someone to exercise this licence with) but there is no evidence in adult married life that this persists—the strictures on adultery applied equally and Levy specifically reports that in Tahiti it is a man's duty to satisfy a woman's sexual needs. She sets the standard; he meets it(61).

It is simply not possible to make a simple assessment of the relative status of men and women for any Polynesian society. The basis of the female strength and security which so many observers have reported probably rests on three major aspects of the female role and the corresponding socialisation which clearly and firmly leads young women toward maturity. These are their economic contribution, their responsibility as household managers, and their biological role as child bearers. In some cases, as in Tonga, it rests also on hereditary status or fixed structural relationships, as with the father's, husband's, or brother's sister who have rank even over males.

In Polynesia women work. They always have done, and they still do. In traditional situations their work is in the gardens and in food production. In Samoa, Hawaii and New Zealand the gathering of shell fish or other food from the reef was a female prerogative. Thus, the collection of special foods, the prized delicacies that Maoris called *kai rangatira*, lay with the women and men were grateful. However, in Samoa, Holmes reported that when the men went bonito fishing, the women and those men not directly involved in the catch were expected to cease their other activities and pray for the success of the fishing, or the fish would not bite; but we must add that our Samoan students had never heard of this! Around the world, when men are doing something that they think is important, women are supposed to stop and pray for them. Who prays for the women? Generally other women. Or no one at all.

While rights to land usually rest with the men, the rights descend through both male and female lines, except in Tonga. The work that produces food from the land is done equally by both men and women but gardens are managed by women. In a sense they belong to them. This economic role of women both limits and balances against the role as child bearer.

As many Polynesian cultures have moved towards a cash economy and wage work, it has been quite natural for women to assume a wage earning role. The mature competence of Tongan women as administrative secretaries is well known in the Pacific and in both of the Samoas women have held important positions such as Director of Education and principal of a teachers' college, something that has yet to happen in New Zealand. The great value of educating women is now widely recognised. Throughout the Pacific there have been prestigious high schools established for girls as well as for boys.

In most parts of Polynesia the traditional form of cooking in earth ovens, the *hangi* or *umu*, was always the preserve of the men. It is they also who make the coconut husk fires along the beach to roast the fresh fish from the catch. Nowadays the ordinary household cooking is more likely to be done by women though Holmes notes that Samoan men still play their part in this area(49). Samoan women, however, seem to be more receptive than the men to both innovative cooking techniques and new foods and recipes.

In Samoa today every village has an active women's committee. These committees have several functions; they have absorbed the traditional role of the *au'uluma* (ceremonial women's group) and the fundraising purpose of women's church associations. In addition women's committees have the job of maintaining and supervising village amenities and often make an economic contribution by means of selling handcrafts or raising poultry. The executive structure of most women's committees follows that of the male status hierarchy of the village so the president is the wife of the highest ranking chief(104).

While the domestic scene is a woman's preserve in the sense that family standing must be protected and displayed in feasts, welcoming relatives, hosting guests and so forth, women are not narrowly confined to domestic roles. For Samoa Mead observed: 'All the irritating, detailed routine of housekeeping, which in our civilization is accused of warping the souls and souring the tempers of grown women, is here performed by children under fourteen years of age'(75, p. 30). That being the case there is ample scope for women to develop other skills.

Prestige positions for women have always been available and important. In Hawaii the *ali'i* (high born) females were not only important in terms of the marriages they could contract but also exercised considerable political power and influence in their own right. There was certainly no political problem in Tonga when Salote became queen, and by her performance of the role she greatly increased the royal *mana*, not only in Tonga but around the world. In New Zealand, the political skill and determination of Te Puea Herangi, the aunt of King Koroki, made her not merely the power behind the king but in her own right a person from whom the *mana* of the royal authority flowed(59). This was not wholly innovative for she had powerful models of effective females both in the history of her tribe and in her own lifetime. Her successor in *mana* is also the *Ariki-nui* in status (paramount chief —the equivalent of king), Dame Te Ata-i-Rangi-Kahu. She ascended to the position in 1966 and has quietly but extremely effectively consolidated the position of the *kingitanga* (kingship) in service to her people. It is quite inappropriate for her to make great public display of what she does but beyond the glare of publicity she has resolutely reformed the basic institutions of the King Movement and modernised it without any loss of its traditional basis. Ten years after her succession the movement is stronger than it has ever been and this is increasingly being recognised by other tribes which in the past have stood somewhat apart from it.

It may seem paradoxical that a society that mostly refuses to allow women to speak on the *marae* (or where one Maori of our acquaintance refuses to work on the ground floor of a building for fear that women will walk over his head and destroy his *tapu*) should also provide the opportunity for a woman to transcend the position of every other male in status terms. Polynesians see no reason at all why they should not have the best of both worlds and what seems like paradoxical conflicts to Pakehas, Palangis or Europeans are for them not problems at all.

Yet it is generally true that Polynesian women have lower life expectancy than European women and in New Zealand a Maori woman, on average, earns less than either a Maori man or a Pakeha woman. Maori women have the highest death rate from lung cancer in the world and very high rates of hypertension. Though certain notable women can and do achieve high prestige and are examples to other women around them, and to those growing up, they are few. These adverse health statistics are a matter of real concern because they indicate that women are being exposed to strains in the modern situation for which their cultural mechanisms of coping are inadequate and with which modern community health services have not even begun to cope.

This is especially true in respect of child bearing and rearing. In a Western society one hardly needs to make this distinction: she who bears also rears and that is that. She may not like it or find it much fun, and it is only recently that Western women have begun to question the bleakness and limitations of their kind of motherhood(14). In Polynesian cultures, it was the duty, the right and the privilege of women to bear children and if they could not they adopted some for it was unthinkable to be a mature woman without a family. Child bearing was the important thing, even if done by proxy. There were plenty of others to attend to the child rearing, and as we have seen, when children grew older, they attended to it themselves. Even today, a successful Polynesian woman may well wish to bear a child or children even though she may be a member of parliament—and after all, why not? Male parliamentarians can enjoy the status of parenthood, of fatherhood, so why should women be forced to give up motherhood for a career—or a career for motherhood? Generalised parenting and child caretakers release women to do other things. But in the modern urban setting, Polynesian women, cut off from community, must bear and rear their children largely unsupported.

There is no recent study of marriage for any Polynesian culture. We wish there were because it is our impression and that of others with whom we talked that in most Polynesian places marriage allows considerably more autonomy to both spouses than is the case in the West. By this we mean that a woman turns to her personal friends, other women, or her family for ordinary companionship, a man to his mates, in a way that places less stress on the exclusive bond between wife and husband. That fits with young adulthood in sex segregated groupings and with the general pattern of community care. Certainly there is less pressure on marriage to 'make it work' because children are looked after whatever happens. We hear reports of wife-beating violence and rape, usually associated with alcohol; we doubt that these are more frequent among Polynesians who drink than among heavy drinkers anywhere.

Whereas in Western society male status depends upon two functions, being a good provider and virility, in the cultures of Polynesia the first is everybody's job and the second more or less taken for granted (except in the case of Tahiti where a pattern of female teasing and joking in the sexual domain probably produces considerable sexual anxiety in men).

In Samoa, Tahiti, Tonga, Honolulu and Pukapuka a few males who fail to measure up to standards of sexual performance can become transvestites, be accepted as such and thus avoid problems of heterosexual anxiety. Levy discusses both the nature and the socialisation processes of such men, termed *mahu* in Tahiti(61). The same pattern is also called *mahu* in Hawaii, *fa'afafine* in the Samoas, *wakawawine* in Pukapuka and *fakaleiti* in Tonga. Anecdotal reports indicate that this is no new phenomenon. A voyager called Mortimer reported *mahu* in Tahiti in 1791(28). Maoris had no word for it but the role probably existed. But even if this was not the case, it certainly exists now, and in a modern context the surrounding society has far more problems coming to terms with the fact and creates considerable problems for the individuals involved. Generally, such men wear women's clothing, engage in their activities, often take on their mannerisms and especially may become skilled dancers and instructors in dance. Sometimes they are also homosexual but not always. They are great devotees of fashion and style and frequently trend-setters. Their presence does not embarrass men or women. In the eyes of women they are helpers and to men they are nothing.

If anxiety about sexual performance is not a conspicuous aspect of the male role, around what do Polynesian cultures elaborate the role definitions for men? The answer lies in two aspects: status in both its ceremonial expression and organisation, and sporting prowess. Both are significant even though occasional in demonstration; they are pervasive and it is through and around them that a male is seen to be good of his kind.

In the Maori situation the reciprocal nature of sex roles can best be seen in those gatherings called *hui* when the hospitality and the entertainment (these days of very large groups, frequently a thousand people or more), clicks into operation smoothly, men and women assuming appropriate tasks but with men, primarily, in the public organising role(103). Some men will be involved in the ceremonies of welcome on the *marae* (generally the elders or *kaumatua*) and though no one is leaping up and shouting instructions and orders the organisation is quietly and efficiently present all the time. Meanwhile, other men will be supervising operations in the kitchens and away collecting food. The role definition, and the satisfaction, is not in the overt act of organising but by participating in a process which is so familiar to everybody that no one need direct it. Still, when a problem arises, everybody knows to whom to turn, and in the last analysis, he is usually male, even if, just behind him, in strength and presence, there is usually a woman.

In Samoan society, the organising role of men is conspicuously seen in the *kava* ceremony, but is also ever present in the day to day running of the household and village activities. This organisational task is coordinated by the *matai* who exercises his authority largely through the male members of the household and village. Samoan agricultural activity is carefully regulated, both to ensure that tasks are done and to minimise thieving and conserve resources. Theft was always a paramount crime in Polynesia, especially from gardens and particularly of prized food such as pineapples or breadfruit. Every food source in every Polynesian environment is owned by someone, even when they appear to be growing free in the wild profusion of a tropical jungle.

It is worth noting that in most of Polynesia, once one leaves the wage-dominated metropolitan centres, one is in a situation that has been described as subsistence or primitive affluence. By this is meant that six to eight hours work overall by the family members will produce enough food for a household for a week if everyone who can works; or so Holmes reports for Ta'u in

American Samoa(49). This means that an hour a day is sufficient to provide all that is necessary, and even less is needed where reef fishing is available and utilised. Holmes notes that the time spent in fishing in Samoa is much less than the Western stereotyped view of island life. In some parts of Polynesia, the Cooks for instance, fishing has virtually ceased to be an important part of the subsistence economy.

Polynesian men have plenty of time to generate all the political activity that seems to be their major preoccupation. While women are often occupied with weaving, making *tapa*, and food preparation, all of these activities are sociable and in the course of them the women monitor the general life of the village. As Levy says of Tahiti, and it is probably true elsewhere, the women are the conscience of the community, keeping an eye on everything that happens, monitoring, guiding, steering, controlling in ways less obvious than those of men but effective none the less.

The best available description of sex roles in any Polynesian culture is contained in Levy's account of Tahiti where, in spite of relative equality between the sexes, both men and women say that women have happier lives(61). Role and task differentiation is clear but not rigid. He reports that at a Western-style dance, if there are not enough women, the young men will dance with other youths. Indeed, they might even do so when there is no shortage of women, simply because they like dancing together and see no reason not to. Levy gives many examples of little ways in which men cross over to take on aspects of the female role and vice versa. As he rightly notes, this is only surprising because it does not happen in Western societies or because the rigid role delineations of the West are not as marked in Polynesian societies. Sex roles in Polynesia are clear—but except in a few special respects, neither obligatory nor exclusive. To be clear is one thing; to be rigid another.

Women in Tahiti may be just as aggressive as men; women are not softer or more maternal than men and both sexes are equally cold towards children when they interfere. Furthermore, it is only the Westerner who expects that people will become anxious if male/female categories become blurred. In many parts of Polynesia women are entitled to initiate sexual intercourse, though not in Tonga nor Samoa where it would be considered brazen or worse. Compared with the West, the grammar of Polynesian languages places little emphasis on gender but simply tacks on the appropriate suffix for male or female where applicable. There is no need to indicate verbally that a pig is a sow when everybody can see; why comment on the obvious? Why use two words when one will do?

Throughout Polynesia, there is relatively little emphasis on sex role differentiation in naming. If you are called Thursday Morning, and someone can't tell by looking at you whether you are male or female, that is their problem. Naming can be this way because the predominant and preferred style of social relationships is familiar and face to face; it is generally not polite to speak of someone who is not present. (Gossiping is something else and is not polite anyway!) And because communication is still primarily oral the ambiguities that arise when one writes things down without indicating gender have not really been thought about. In an oral tradition, non-verbal cues are ever present and provide the glosses that indicate gender.

All this may be changing and many of the changes may not be for the better. At this time people in Polynesia, even in remote locations, need to be thinking about how modernisation is affecting the traditional balance of complementarity between the sex roles of male and female.

Many things which are not thought of as part of sex roles affect them. For example, the community needs to provide the same kinds of support for both men and women who wish to go away to improve their skills and qualifications or to earn money to contribute to their community on the island. There is no reason at all why working women should not continue to be child bearers, since in Polynesia there are plenty of caretakers for the children. In particular, both men and women should watch most carefully for the importation of Western ideas in areas such as medicine and education. Often these are implicitly but heavily loaded with antiquated Western conceptions of sex role appropriate behaviour. For example, Western women are fighting now to wrest from male doctors and technicians the control of the experience of labour and birth. In Polynesia birth was always in the hands of women, regardless of what men may think. Western men, through modern legislative process have the means of control, and in New Zealand anyway, have imposed their will on women's reproductive functioning.

When women go in for wage work, other women should be organising so that they share in the economic wage benefits by following Polynesian tradition and assuming responsibility for children other than their own. When someone goes out to work, everyone who stays behind must work a little harder in the gardens or else the cultivated land will return to jungle and its productivity be lost to everyone. Nowhere in the Pacific is the wage economy so stable and secure that the subsistence base can be forgotten and left behind. So long as some contribution is coming back to the community from the wage work of everybody, at home or abroad, the Polynesian virtue of sharing in sex roles as in everything else will be maintained.

The traditional conception of female beauty and the proper display of female attractiveness is effective in its own cultural terms and while Western women are, increasingly, rejecting their treatment as sex objects in the media and as promoters of consumption in advertising, there is utterly no reason that the women of Polynesia should be sucked into the same trap. A bikini is not any more alluring than a *pareu*, and it is a lot less comfortable. Western hair straighteners and bleaches have never caught on in Polynesia (though bleaching was traditional in some places) but ridiculous shoes with high platform soles have, and can do more than simply distort physical deportment and grace by causing physical damage to the body's alignment. Polynesians would do well to insist on the retention of their own dress styles, bare feet and so on, adapting these only in the interests of practicality.

Since both men and women participate in the care of the very young child the development of appropriate sex role behaviour seems no great or complex one. Children have many appropriate models. The way the roles are built up, then played, allocates functions differently from the West and generally there are more cultural supports for women to become politically active and effective—but only at a local level (with some exceptions as we indicated earlier). It has been noted for Samoa that though few women are *matai* (chiefs) every Samoan woman has the right to make her views known when titles are being conferred(104). Thus women have influence in the power structure of their society, though few are able to exercise this power directly.

Complementary these sex roles may be but equal they are not. In the past the question of equality has, perhaps, not been of great account but those times have gone. Women have not yet entered the political arena, in meaningful numbers or terms, anywhere in Polynesia. The status positions, the wealth, the power, lie mostly with men. Perhaps this may begin to change as Polynesian women reassess for themselves the consequences of this complementary but unequal situation.

More than in any other aspect the two sexes will need to work out some rational allocation of responsibility in respect of breeding. The health of women is a serious concern and we suspect that the ill health of women relates to too many pregnancies at too small an interval. Obesity, bad diet and cigarette smoking are the other contributing facts and all are related to a life style that puts reproduction so high on the priority list of female functions and duties that until something is done about it the situation will get worse, not better.

There is evidence that some women are beginning to realise this but very very few men are. Tubal ligation is not infrequent among Maori women who want to cease child-bearing; vasectomy is virtually unknown among men. However much one may find evidence of complementarity in other matters there is little in this: the pattern of Polynesian population growth is being maintained by men, at the expense of the health and welfare of women, and in the last analysis to the social and environmental detriment of both. Epeli Hau'ofa speaks of Tonga: 'Within a few decades our environment will not support the quality of life that we have known for generations. Should this occur, the continuity between ourselves and our ancestors which has been the cornerstone of our identity as people will be broken. We will then become a nation without a past, without a soul, without a future'(47, p. 34), and the whole of his brief but eloquent paper sees unrestrained breeding as the final impact that will destroy the Tongan way of life. The same is true for any island people.

Polynesian men may protest that the ideas of women's liberation are yet another foreign piece of Western devilry but Polynesian women, especially the younger ones, will not accept that. They are beginning to tell their own story(45). Oppression is oppression, everywhere, and women are oppressed in Polynesian cultures not so much by traditional roles as by what has happened to them over time and in modern contexts. Whether they are as oppressed as their sisters elsewhere is a pointless comparison. Complementarity will hardly suffice in a world where equality is not merely a slogan but a right.

CHAPTER *11*

Early Education

'I don't agree that children should go to preschool. The Western idea is to get rid of children as quickly as possible. Why should a child hurry so much at the expense of his enjoyment? He can always finish a year or two later. After all, people come to universities even when they are quite old.'
'Preschools can create greater inequalities. Everyone can't afford to send their children to preschool as it is even more expensive than sending them to primary school.'
'In my own childhood there were no preschools as really there was no need for them. However, nowadays, the fact that both parents have to work (particularly in urban centres), has led to the sudden development of so many preschools. It is interesting to note that in most cases parents have minimal contact with the preschool since they are working full time. Thus, as long as their children are attending a preschool centre, they are contented, regardless of what type of learning is going on.'
'My little girl is attending a well equipped kindergarten but she has learnt nothing much beyond socialising with the other children. In fact, I think she has lost much which she had learnt at home in terms of language structures and vocabulary. I have often wondered what they are being taught or supposed to learn.'

Up to this point we have chiefly been concerned with the cultural continuities of home, family and village where, largely through incidental learning, the ground plan of being Polynesian is established. In this and later chapters we will be concerned with some dominant but less traditional influences on child development in the Pacific. Whereas in the past few formal institutions for education existed in the area, Western style schooling has come, is valued and certainly will not go away again. There is no debate, really, about the value of primary, secondary and tertiary schooling. Everywhere except in Hawaii, New Zealand and American Samoa resources are still so limited that not all get to primary school (though Tonga has compulsory primary schooling), fewer to secondary and only the very best to university, technical institutes, theological or teachers' colleges.

But there is still a little reservation about extending education downward. Some of this doubt is based on economic grounds—how much schooling can a developing country afford?—some derives from real doubt that early education is worthwhile; some from a belief that women should do it in the home and preschools will undermine the role of parents, home and village.

In our view, once there are schools, preschools are needed but before we come to discuss this we need to consider some background facts.

We cannot find much evidence that, in traditional times, young children were expected to learn anything at all apart from what they learned in their participation in the daily life of the people. That is to say, there was no self-conscious concept of what a child needs to know or when it is ready to learn. Learning, in the sense of instruction, certainly did occur when young men in particular were initiated into the more formal statuses of ceremonial participation, and Frisbee remarks upon his stumbling across old ladies instructing young girls in dance ceremonial late at night(36). The instruction of young women in women's houses is more characteristic of Micronesian cultures than of Polynesian where in dancing and in weaving the learning took place informally by example and imitation, rather than by direct instruction. In Tonga the preparation of the children of the nobility and especially of the royal family received special attention.

Though the status of the ethnographic record has been questioned, contemporary Maori people certainly believe that there were traditional schools of instruction convened from time to time to pass on a particular body of knowledge such as that which relates to cosmological conceptions (the work of the gods) or canoe carving or schools of magic for healing or other purposes. But all this was for adults, sometimes of quite advanced age.

Not only was there no traditional concept of early education in Polynesia, but even today its necessity may be debated, particularly when it is presented in terms of the Western tradition where education through play has become the prevailing basis for early education facilities. The debate is not among parents who, everywhere, want their children to succeed and see preschool as the first step, but among those who see it as another cost or who do not want money deflected from their part of the education system.

We have heard Maori elders, and mothers, talk scornfully about the free play approach, and their opinion was formed by their own direct experience. If there is to be preschooling they want it to be a serious matter and they don't believe that education through free play is really education at all. On one occasion we heard a Department of Education Preschool Adviser advocating experience in the sand pile as the only early learning needed—to parents whose children played all day in the sand dunes that surrounded and nearly swamped the village. Because they see free play as plentifully available at home they want something more from preschools, and they are not very convinced by arguments that learning through play is better than learning any other way.

Whatever the traditional situation may have been, Polynesian parents nowadays want their children to receive early education that will be of help to them at school. And this requires much more than just playing with sand. For New Zealand we know what it is that Maori mothers want for their children, and primarily this is that children shall learn social and educational skills that will help them at school(67, 68, 95, 96).

Western traditions of preschool education tend to be very child-centered. Simply by providing an appropriate environment learning will unfold as though pre-programmed within the young child. Now, some learning by young children does seem to be like that. Children learn to talk seemingly without much in the way of direct instruction but in fact, unless children are surrounded by good language models and by people who shape and correct their language behaviour, they will not become very articulate, even in their own tongue. The psychology of early development is very clear on this matter—unless children are stimulated in particular ways their interest is not aroused and learning is not sustained. Even at the earliest age purposeful instruction is worthwhile. The Maori proverb, 'grow tender plant in the days of thy youth', may be beautiful poetry, but is bad psychology. People are not plants, they do not grow well when simply left alone.

There are four basic modern models for preschool systems. We mention them because they are the models which are likely to be influencing the development of preschool education in the Pacific.

The first is the 'learning-through-play' model which advocates the provision of copious equipment, the 'rich play environment' through which the child is expected to make his or her own way, learning being somehow presumed to occur by magic along the way. After years of trying we still do not understand the learning theory on which this is based. Rather, we think that children in this sort of environment learn very little that they would not learn were they never to enter a preschool, and often become bored. Indeed it may be that by learning inattention, by not being trained in listening, watching, observing and in language skills, this sort of preschooling may develop a sort of random, butterfly, whim-directed kind of activity that may interfere with later learning.

This play tradition is loaded with Western family style assumptions concerning the necessity for parent involvement, the need for continuing close contact of the child with the mother, the need to provide a child from a small family with company of his or her own age. In our view the organisation of preschool education in this way has largely developed to provide middle class children with experiences to compensate for those of which they are deprived in their small, nuclear, urban family environments. Even where the advocates of this style have tried to apply their ideology and techniques to the needs of ethnic minorities in New Zealand, the Polynesian cultural component is thin, poorly understood, ineffectual and trivial, an overlay that makes little contact with the core of cultural values.

The second model includes a number of different ideas which developed in a number of different places but all of which centre around the basic idea that by providing carefully structured play experiences children somehow hook onto progressions in basic learning. The name of Maria Montessori is most clearly associated with this and her ideas have led to the setting up of some interesting experimental schools but basically the stress is still on the equipment and on free progressions through play. To help the child use this equipment the Montessori method requires a skilled teacher trained in the appropriate techniques. The value of this approach lies in its emphasis on the provision of structure in the immediate environment. But it lacks recognition of the essentially verbal nature of concept learning. With blocks and dough and containers and water and sand children may well develop some interesting understandings of the physical way the world works and no doubt enjoy many tactile experiences, but without language they will not be able to tell anyone about them, nor be able really to think about them. They may acquire concepts of quantity and size but until they start to talk about these as ideas the essentially social and cultural nature of what one does with concepts fails to progress.

We have come to the conclusion, for reasons that we will explain shortly, that whatever the culture, what young children need is a rich environment of verbal understanding and experience(106) —and not just playing with things. Words, in any language, are the tools whereby the social world becomes intelligible to the young child and he or she learns then to operate within it.

The third model has arisen through such programmes as Project Head Start in the United States and constitutes a downward extension back into home and community of the idea of school as a place where learning occurs, where children are taught, where they begin to develop the cultural and therefore linguistic basis of their heritage.

Head Start began as a programme to compensate for the disadvantage suffered by urban American, largely ethnic minority group children, but it is most unfortunate that the value of it as a systematic approach to early education has been caught up in the concept of disadvantage. No one with any pride will readily accept that their child is disadvantaged, but anyone can recognise that preschools should prepare children for school. Along the way, a good preschool will do much more than this. Preparing a child for school does not imply that the parents have somehow been deficient and allowed their child to become disadvantaged. But as we have said, schools are a new and Western part of Polynesian life and though they may change to be less so they still require behaviour patterns and skills for which there is no traditional model or institution of learning in Polynesia. We may be wrong about this. But we know that Polynesian parents and communities endorse the kinds of training of behaviour that programmes such as Head Start attempted to teach.

Indeed we know that this is so because of the strong endorsement in the recent past, in Tonga, of a fourth model derived from old mission-style education, almost like the old dame school that Beeby has written about(10). The rigid regimentation of learning with strong emphasis on rote learning, the chorussing of information and an organisation that kept children occupied largely on the mat singing hymns and chanting ABCs was not likely to achieve the same behavioural objectives as programmes like Head Start. So let us return to these and discuss them.

The first objective is confidence. Children who have a positive view of themselves are likely to have successful learning experiences. So the preschool should endeavour to send the children off to school knowing they can be successful learners with a good self concept, ready to cope with life at school.

Secondly, to be successful at school, children need to be attentive listeners and observers rather than flitting from here to there, playing with this or that. So, without being dour about it, the preschool can sit them down from time to time in small groups and train their attention, gradually lengthening the span, to show them how to attend to detail, to stay on a task until the job is done.

Thirdly, in Polynesia where the cultures require it they need to recognise the authority and status of the teacher and the respect that is due to the teaching person. This means listening closely to what the teacher says, following instructions and asking for help when needed. Given the background of Polynesian socialisation, this may be difficult for some children because they have learned already to solve their own problems in the peer situation rather than by turning to adults for assistance. However, in the more stratified societies, Samoa and Tonga for example, neither children nor parents have any trouble accepting that the teacher is an authority deserving of respect. Gallimore and his colleagues and Howard identified a very important and common kind of behaviour in Hawaiian children, that we know occurs elsewhere, which consists of the child standing silently with an imploring look sending body language messages that he or she needs help, waiting to be noticed but not able to ask(38, 52). Children have to learn to make their needs known verbally. This is one of those obvious things that many people overlook because they think children all ask questions naturally. Some of course do, but a shy child or a child whose socialisation has not encouraged such behaviour will need to be taught and encouraged. In Polynesia there are areas of life that children are not supposed to ask questions about, indeed direct questioning is regarded as rather rude almost everywhere and so before they recognise what those areas are they may learn not to ask questions at all. They will not do well at school that way.

In traditional societies one's language is developed through bursts of development followed by long plateaus. You need only a very simple, direct and limited vocabulary to get along in peer groups and make your needs known. And that will do for years and years. But when at adolescence the language of status and respect is required a whole new development of language takes place. In Samoa, Mead noted this applied especially to males(75).

The existence of the school, which has its own kind of language, needs prior language learning. Beyond this is the increasing complexity of language which surrounds modern Polynesian children through the media and the intrusion of influences from beyond the island. If the child is going to deal with this aspect of life at all, having adequate language becomes very important indeed. New concepts which are part of the modern world relating to science, industry, horticulture, conservation, energy, have to become part of the child's language even if at very low levels of sophistication or children will indeed be deprived of the opportunity to understand what is going on around them even on the most remote atoll. Even the changes taking place in the development of political systems, and these are happening everywhere in Polynesia, have produced new complexities in the social world.

In all Polynesian traditions the power of language is appreciated and the word is sacred. Respect for language is an important consideration everywhere in Polynesia. In an oral tradition it must be so and few cultures have developed oratory and poetry to the heights which they reached in Polynesia. In oratory Polynesians have an appreciation of verbal subtlety and wit that leave most Westerners sounding like inarticulate fools. Westerners really no longer have a tradition of oratory at all. The metaphors, puns, mythic allusions, make Polynesian languages, at least in their high stylistic forms, more like English poetry than prose. All that needs to be learned. Therefore there is every reason why an emphasis on language should be a central part of Polynesian preschooling, a major focus of attention.

A good preschool programme will also place considerable emphasis on books. Because Polynesian cultures had not invented literacy the socialisation supports for reading and writing never developed. But they are there now. Before reading can begin there are many 'bookish' things that need to be learned. The first is the realisation that all those funny marks can be transformed into those sounds, the one-to-one correspondence between the print and the word. Along with this a fine perceptual tuning is required to recognise the pattern distinctions between words and letters. Thirdly is the recognition that all those little black and white patterns contain ideas that you do not yet know about, and therefore that print is a path to knowledge. That realisation trips the motivational trigger that makes books something of value and reading an enjoyable and self-enhancing activity. Along with these are the sheer mechanical things; learning which way on the page is up, the front and back of a book, and the left to right eye sweep which is customary in Western print, eye return from the bottom of a page to the top of the next. Because books are a human invention they are not part of nature. Nothing in nature trains you to sweep your eye from left to right. There is nothing natural about reading and it will not naturally arise; it has to be taught. You won't learn that in the sand pit. In some Polynesian cultures where children are introduced early to the singing of hymns and the reading of the Bible, there are already some socialisation supports for reading as an activity, but we know that human beings everywhere need to receive this pre-reading training between the second and the sixth year if the development of reading is to progress smoothly(23). We will discuss the techniques of this shortly.

Books have a story to tell. The story of the book is constant; it becomes familiar, well-loved. Similarly they evoke constant emotions and moods; the pleasures are assured, the fears familiar and safe. Reading is an active exchange between the book and the reader's mind and emotions. Each experience with each book is a significant event.

Perhaps the most important change that Head Start programmes introduced into the early education field was the idea of curriculum, that is, a course of instruction or a set of clear ideas about what it is that children shall learn. To many people the idea that little children should be subjected to something bearing such an imposing name as a curriculum seems unnecessary, unnatural and maybe even harmful. A syllabus of instruction sounds very formidable and laden with menace of examinations and such like. But if you don't know what you're aiming for, how do you know when you've got there? And even more important, how do the children know when they have got there? A curriculum involves nothing more than setting out what you hope to teach in an orderly way so that you can then provide the children with the learning experiences that achieve those understandings. Once you have a curriculum, however simple that may be, then it becomes easy to apply an evaluation to assess the success of what you are doing.

In the play oriented preschool style, no one knows exactly what the children are supposed to be learning, no one knows if they have learned it and little effort is made to find out. It is all too easy for such a preschool to slip into mere time-filling—'cutting up egg-cartons' a friend of ours calls it—and the 'teacher', if there is one, becomes merely the inventor of yet another round of 'things to do', none of which add up to anything much. In structured preschooling, by contrast, whatever the language of instruction may be, children can learn that there are words for big and small, fat and thin, colour names, prepositions like in, on, under, adjectival extensions of the meaning of nouns as well as matters of etiquette and social behaviour, all of which constitute the curriculum. While some children may learn such things anyway others do not—or do not learn them before they go to school.

But some argue that children can be left to learn things later and that preschooling is taking away some vague and ill-defined heritage of childhood. By our nature the human species, above all other living things, is equipped to learn. We learn best from another human being, not by being left to scratch like chickens for whatever knowledge we may glean. We progress, as we learn how to learn, from being dependent on one person as teacher, to learning in small groups, then in larger groups, and as we go along gradually we acquire more and more skill at autonomous learning. Mostly we learn from our successes, not our failures, and from rewards, not punishments.

Consider now how the Polynesian pattern reflects this sequence: At first the child has warm one-to-one relationships with many nurturant adults; then he or she graduates to the small groups of peers and siblings; then to school. The preschool can reflect this sequence too if it brings in adults enough to provide plenty of one-to-one learning and lots of chances for children to learn in groups. Children can be taught, and must be taught what people in their society value—language, skills, social manners and practices, how to express their emotions, whatever they need.

When we came to start on our own preschool project with Maori children, Te Kohanga, we tried to put these ideas into practice.

From the many different kinds of Head Start early education projects, including experiments in this direction with Hawaiian children and Aboriginal children, a common element was that a full time professional person directed the programme(54, 83). This, we can now see, was not absolutely necessary and in the context of the Polynesian environments not always possible. The principles upon which Head Start programmes were based can be operated in a village setting by parent cooperative groups using skills which already exist among local residents. This is already happening in American Samoa, Western Samoa and Tonga and the future looks promising.

In New Zealand early education gets the scrapings from the bottom of the financial barrel: its teachers are poorly paid, low in status (compared with other teachers) and receive one year less training than primary teachers. We would advocate that preschool education be recognised as the foundation of learning. It seems wasteful to provide money more lavishly at the top end of the scale while the early foundations are starved. On the other hand, there are very good reasons why early education should be provided on a community cooperative basis and an artificial barrier between school and community avoided. The teachers should be community teachers looking to both child and adult education.

For a number of years New Zealand has had provision for attaching a preschool to a regular primary school. We do not see why this should not be done everywhere, especially since in most Polynesian locations a primary school is already located within the community whose school it is, rather than belonging to the government.

Since it is closest in our own experience we would like to illustrate what we have been saying by describing the workings of our own experimental preschool for Maori children, Te Kohanga.

It was begun under the auspices of the Centre for Maori Studies and Research of the University of Waikato. It ran for three years and its programmes have been fully reported(95, 96). This project sought to identify skills which are related to success at school and then to teach them to Maori four-year-olds. Thus they would be able to enter school ready to profit from the activities there right away without a period of adjustment.

The programme had four structural planks: experiences, books, language and concepts, and developmental activities. The last of these was the opportunity for free play in a rich environment as found in any New Zealand preschool. It occupied more than half of each of the five morning sessions. Visits extended the experiences of the children, most of whom had never been to such places as a farm, a zoo, or even a supermarket. These visits were the basis of the curriculum. When we systematically studied the language of these children the full extent of their limitations became clear: they had no names for parts of their body like feet and toes, for common animals like horse, cow and sheep, for colours or foods like peas and corn. So extending their vocabulary was one of the first objectives of the language programme.

Literacy is a fundamental skill so we wanted the Te Kohanga

children to enter school with a good foundation for it. This included a familiarity with books, strong and favourable attitudes to them, and the basic skills that a child must have before he or she learns to read. Each child took a book home every night for home story reading. The classics of children's literature were read over and over again to develop and fix language patterns. A new story was read daily without fail to every child, either individually or in small groups, and books formed the basis of a systematic language extension programme. The book programme is fully reported by Nancy Gerrand(39).

While books are available in kindergartens and play centres in New Zealand and elsewhere, they are used for story reading only, rather than for systematic language instruction. They are not exploited as they might be if preschools became more actively places where people teach and children learn.

This was an elaborate experimental research project. It was also very expensive. It was not established as a model for others to copy, but aimed to test some new ideas and to challenge the assumptions and prevailing idealogy of existing preschool institutions in New Zealand. It met a need; it did establish good school foundations for the children and there is absolutely no doubt that the Maori parents recognised in it exactly what they wanted for their children, for whom going to preschool and then to school was a highly positive experience in which they discovered the pleasure of learning. Visitors from other Polynesian cultures were also impressed with the programme and felt that with suitable modification some of the ideas and practices could be widely applied.

An immediate and apparent problem in any preschool programme in Polynesia is the almost total absence of suitable preschool books. We recognise the same lack in Maori language books here in New Zealand. There are two ways of overcoming this. The first is simply to use the ordinary published story books and paste the appropriate local language translation over the text. But this requires the initial purchase of shop books which are expensive. The more creative and therefore the preferred alternative is to produce your own books, writing simple local stories and illustrating them with simple line drawings. Almost anyone can write a story and very little skill is needed to draw the pictures. The best models, readily available and well known, illustrate some of the features children enjoy such as repetition (*Three Little Pigs*), rhythm and rhyme (Stan and Jan

Berenstain's series about Bears), humour and drama (*Bears in the Night*), rich vocabulary (*Where the Wild Things Are*), racy story line (*Gingerbread Man*) and familiar language patterns (*Three Bears*). Anyone who reflects on the stories they loved as a child can find the principles of good writing for children in any language. Books can be produced very cheaply by Gestetner or jelly pad or even by hand-made single copies, the pages stapled or sewn together. Katarina Mataira of the Centre for Maori Studies and Research at the University of Waikato has run local workshops for interested people who have had great fun producing an exciting and useful little series of early reading books in Maori.

Counting, sorting, matching, colour naming skills can all be taught using local materials such as shells, seeds, flowers and leaves. Off-cut blocks can be trimmed to standard sizes and used for building blocks, cans from the kitchen can be used for measuring and stacking. We have to face it: governments just aren't going to fund preschools liberally, anywhere, so pragmatic use must be made of what is available.

Around the Pacific various ways of organising preschool education have developed. Here are some examples. Western Samoa has a flourishing preschool movement; the Western Samoa Preschool Association was formed in 1971. There are now 60 preschool centres operating, with plans for a further 60, catering at present for 4000 of the country's 10 000 preschool children. The preschools are village-based and staffed by voluntary teachers, trained by the association. Villages provide the land, buildings and the equipment. The association stresses that the style of preschooling offered in Samoa must meet the needs of the Samoan child. Preschooling is intended both to prepare a child for further education and to teach the child to become a good Samoan. Thus there is a curriculum that stresses both academic skills such as concept learning and the learning of the *Fa'a Samoa*, the Samoan way of life. The daily programme allows both for free play activities and for set learning periods.

The Tonga Preschool Association, though it operates on a smaller scale, is also a soundly based and vigorous organisation coordinating the activities of about 16 preschool centres. It facilitates the training of its teachers by supervising and supplementing the assignments required for New Zealand Play Centre Association qualifications. Preschooling is largely village-based and it is suggested that the fees paid by each child should allow for a modest wage to be paid to each teacher. Tongan parents favour a strong academic basis in their children's preschool education and the association finds that it must resist strong parental pressure for a constant daily programme of set lessons unleavened by free choice activities.

Fiji has about 120 preschools, catering for 1300 children, approximately 15 per cent of the preschool age group(105). Most preschools are in urban centres and are organised by private organisations, such as church and ethnic groups, who may run a preschool as an adjunct to their primary school. Equipment is not lavish and the children have plenty of opportunity for free play. Parents must pay and the teachers receive a small wage. A few preschools, known as 'schools of nine' (nine is the number that a person can teach without requiring a licence) have a more academic orientation. These are run by expatriates catering mainly for expatriate children. The Education Department has two preschool advisers whose function is to ensure that minimal standards are met and to provide brief courses (one week to one month) for preschool teachers.

Whatever may be the prevailing climate of adult–child relationships outside the preschool, it is very important that if children are to learn from adults they must be seen not as powerful and punishing but as positive people who praise and reward. It is our experience that young Polynesian children are more than willing to relate to adults who give them some attention and this willingness is an asset that can be used by the teaching people in a preschool setting. There is no need to advocate some great change in parent–child relationships nor to disturb the Polynesian ordering of these as lots of praise, lots of attention, and a genuine warmth will go a long way. To this must be added a practical firmness so that children learn when it is time for relaxation and when it is time for serious concentration.

Though we cannot cite references to support our contention we think it very likely that the free play environment does very little to support, develop or promote respect for adults. It may in fact do the opposite. Respect is so vital a part of the Polynesian view of social relationships that we think that Polynesians would want it to be expressed in every part of every learning situation. We know Maori parents who have been horrified at high school teachers so young in outlook that they have, so to speak, joined the gang of their classroom rather than reflecting into it the proper relationship of respect that older people should expect from younger people and that younger people should show to those older than them.

As we have seen, strong development of preschooling is already taking place in the Samoas, in Fiji, in Tonga and Niue and may need little more than to be supported in the right direction. In Samoa so well trained are graduates of the training programme of the preschool association that they are already much in demand as primary school teachers of new entrant classes. Whatever more is done in preschooling will have to be undertaken without great demands upon the public purse and largely through the utilisation and development of the skills of people already living in the communities and villages. But there is a strong sense among the people of the value of early education and demand for it.

We have heard people say that community preschools often start, run for a time and then fizzle out and we are prepared to believe that this is the case, for we know the effort needed to sustain them. Why should this be so? It may be that people in the community need to be constantly reminded about how important preschool learning really is. It may be that from time to time the high status people of the community need to be reminded of their obligation to show their support for the preschool. Educational cooperatives are always at risk where they depend upon one person too much. Such a person might move away, lose interest, have a tiff with someone in the community or feel unrecognised or unrewarded. It may be that those involved simply lose faith because what they are doing is not sufficiently structured for them to see the value of the progress that the children are making. Without structure and guidance the aimlessness and formlessness simply becomes unrewarding for everyone. And where the school does not help and support, the preschool morale slumps.

Often where a preschool had begun through someone's enthusiasm the bureaucratic demands placed upon that effort defeat it. Sometimes these are official—building requirements, things needed before a subsidy is granted; sometimes they arise within voluntary associations. Finding one's way through the maze of requirements of the New Zealand Play Centre Association's stipulations concerning equipment, mother helping, parent training, provision of play areas, is very daunting to anyone wanting to set up something for their local children.

Whatever is done for preschooling in Polynesia needs to be done so that preschooling is seen to be part of the whole pattern of education in school and out of school, reflecting community, cultural and children's needs.

As we have discussed the major themes of childhood in the cultures of Polynesia we have not sought for some outlandish, exotic or special set of characteristics. Rather we have seen how these cultures place an emphasis on some feature at each stage and pace or punctuate development so that some attributes develop more quickly at one time than another. In a similar way we would suggest that preschooling does not need to be radically different from elsewhere but needs to reflect the major features of Polynesian style.

The language should be the language of the locality, with English coming in only as a skill language for school-related content like counting or not even being used at all, according to parental preference. The degree of formality/informality is quite optional though it is hard to run a curriculum or a structured language programme without some degree of formality.

In its organisation the preschool, if it is to be a learning setting and not just child minding or play activity, cannot simply replicate the peer and sibling play groups of Pacific childhood, yet the three-year-olds can work in their groups while the fours do other things together. And if there are enough adults interested, involved and attending regularly, ways might be found of including all children of any age, especially if the under-threes can be provided with lots of free play in the equivalent of a crèche situation. That a preschool should be for everyone not at school is a rather nice idea.

Again we repeat that we are not out to provide answers but simply to create an awareness. But, to be quite honest, we do have a preference; we would like to see each Polynesian culture continuing to develop its own range and variety of preschooling experiments, some in villages, some in towns, all pooling ideas together so that what is done reflects both the particular locality and culture, and the general style of Polynesian childhood.

CHAPTER *12*

School and Community

'The mana of any school depends so much on the number of passes in the external examinations. This means teaching in the classroom is geared to the examinations and both students and teachers are overworked. Promotion of primary teachers in Tonga depends on the students passing the external examinations.'

'School is often referred to by Samoan parents as a way to a "good life", meaning a "soft" way of earning a living in terms of cash as compared to collecting coconuts, drying them into copra before selling them to traders before any kinds of goods can be obtained. This is the "hard way", our parents said. If one wanted to end up in such a way, then be a truant. It seemed to me to be more of a threat than advice.'

'Fiji parents seem to want academically-orientated with strong examination bias-type schools for their children. I think only when the employing sector of the community stops insisting on exam passes as criteria for job eligibility will the parents consider other types of education.'

'We were sent to school to read, write and to speak English. This was to be the ticket for a "better life". I don't think either of my parents knew much more about school or its function beyond it being a tool for literacy. However, I think it was an unvoiced assumption that no matter what happened at school we would still learn to be Fijians.'

'My secondary education was a hard and challenging time. Both my parents had passed away and so I had financial problems. I had to rely mostly on what my paternal uncle could provide and he had to look after his own four children. My oldest sister had to quit school in order to work and support the rest of us. Most of the money that went into my education came from fundraising in my community.'

School, as a special place provided by adults where children are to be instructed, was invented only twice in human history, among the Hebraic tribes of the Middle East and in the Bhuddist tradition of Central Asia. From each of those two centres the idea of school, the institution, spread around the world. In both cases schools were established for the transmission of sacred and scriptural knowledge and practices. In most parts of the world, over most of human history, children were needed to work in field and farms and in hunting, gathering and herding. Survival depended on it. Even when people knew about school, the idea did not always make sense.

Nor did it immediately in Polynesia. The missionaries who brought the Western model of schooling found adults were interested right away; literacy was a new and seemingly practical kind of magic, so that schools for adults spread and literacy was a new kind of status marker. But that such benefits should be bestowed on children was not at all immediately apparent and the missionaries often had to go out and round the children up for themselves.

In some ways it is strange that the idea of schools had not been invented spontaneously in Polynesian societies prior to the advent of European contact. All the ingredients were there—for example, age graded associations of children, available adult labour with time to spare, the obvious desire of adults to have the children occupied or separated from adult activity, a body of traditional knowledge of various kinds the transmission of which was a matter of concern.

Indeed, in New Zealand the Maori schools for learning esoteric knowledge, the *whare wananga*, were schools in most respects but applied to only a narrow age range of the adult male population and were for the transmission of very specialised knowledge. They operated only occasionally, as the need arose, and were exclusively for selected young aristocrats. Their equivalent is the idea of a university, not the school of mass education that developed after the industrial revolution in Europe.

In other aspects of learning in many parts of Polynesia the idea of adults taking time and being allowed time by the community to instruct the young was recognised and valued, as when women teach young girls the intricacies of weaving traditional patterns and designs. In finite terms there is not a lot of knowledge of this kind to be transmitted in any Polynesian culture, well developed though these crafts were. Though master navigators took on apprentices this was neither as formal nor developed in Polynesia as in Micronesia where ocean navigation was much more a way of life(41). In such matters as *kava* celebrations young men needed to learn customs, conduct and ceremonies, but this was done in cultural context, not in a school.

So the cultural situation was ripe everywhere when the missionaries arrived and began schools. And the cultural acceptance was ready and enthusiastic. Not everybody wanted to be a convert but everybody wanted to go to school and literacy spread like an infectious disease throughout the Pacific. It is interesting to note the purposes to which it was put once it was obtained. The picture is sketchy and incomplete, and the matter needs to be researched, but in both New Zealand and Hawaii there were three major uses for the new-found literacy.

The first and most obvious was to get access to the sacred word of the European and it was not only the missionary who desired the early Bible translation into the native language. Here was access to the book which was the basis of European magic. The word-magic of the Bible clearly bestowed status and prestige upon the missionaries in relation to other Europeans and it contained legends and stories parallel to and having very similar emotional effect as those of Polynesian myth. Here were new possible cultural revelations, possibly new words from the ancestors. It was a route to a new kind of supernatural power; it bestowed *mana*. For this literacy was fervently required.

The second area, for which we have copious existing documentation, is economic. Through literacy supplication could be made, orders sent, tallies kept of the goods which once they knew, Polynesians wanted. One collection of letters held by our own university (Waikato), written to Bishop Selwyn by chiefs of high status throughout central New Zealand, read like a collection of shopping lists: 'Sir, we would like three pairs of breeding pigs, twelve shovels, ten sacks of seed corn', and so on. The missionaries had access to the goodies and literacy seemed to be one way to get at them. The parable of the talents, much preached to promote Christian industry, met a ready audience which just needed the wherewithal to get started.

But other letters and similar documents also contain a great expression of concern about the disruptive effects of the European presence, and also reports on the possible threats from other chiefs and tribes around the letter-writer's area. Increasingly, as time goes on, they become anxious appeals to governors or to government, urgently pleading that controls be established to stop rum-running, land-grabbing and similar lawlessness, sometimes powerful and accurate political analyses, so that literacy was also a route to power, a way of expressing respect, of manipulating status and thereby attaining peace and security or advantage over rivals.

Where did you acquire literacy? At school, that's where. Whatever the situation in the past, there is no question now but that Polynesians want their children to go to school, see the school as the place where they will become educated and see education as a way of getting ahead. From time to time, some may have questioned the value of schools, particularly recently as it has become fashionable to point to the hidden curriculum of Western value assumptions implicit in the way schools are organised and the kind of knowledge they regard as of value. But these modern critics never get far because Polynesian parents know what schools are for—learning skills useful in the modern world.

We know of only one serious endeavour to reject European schooling on a large scale and that was when King Tawhiao at the close of the Waikato Land Wars in New Zealand warned his people to stay clear of Pakeha education. Defeated in war, driven into exile and their lands seized, the Waikato could have become bitter and dispirited. Tawhiao, twenty years later, was urging his people to self-sufficiency as a route to social reconstruction(72). He meant them to set up their own courts and councils and to reject European influence by refusing to pay rates, sell land or send their children to Pakeha schools. But even this injunction is more powerful as a legend than a case of fact. Throughout the Waikato most children still went to school though the children of some aristocratic families did not (and by this, perhaps, seriously jeopardised the effectiveness of the King movement) for over half a century. It took the innovative force of a personally charismatic member of the leadership, Te Puea Herangi, to restore the endorsement of education; immediately that was done all the people sought it with as much enthusiasm as anywhere else. Te Uira Manihera thinks Tawhiao really intended that the people set up their own schools, and maybe they did for a time but by the turn of the century the wounds were healing(72). Children were going to school.

With this early and continuous cultural endorsement why is it that children do not always do as well as their parents expect? To answer this we need to look in greater detail at how education systems have evolved and how they relate to the pattern of Polynesian socialisation described earlier, at the fit between the school and its institutional history and the person and his or her life history.

We do not propose, nor are we able, to write a comprehensive survey of everything that has happened in education in the Pacific nor to undertake a close comparative look at contemporary Pacific educational systems. However, there have been great changes in the last decade as Pacific countries have taken control of their own education destinies and begun to modernise the colonial systems which they inherited so that schooling will reflect the local cultural aspirations. Mele Waqa(114) provides information about educational provision in Fiji and for facts and figures about school systems in any Pacific place consult the relevant sections of the Pacific Islands Yearbook(87). But schooling is everywhere a part of the business of growing up so we must ask what is its role in the kind of socialisation we have been discussing and its effects on family life-styles.

Some aspects of the way schools have developed must be mentioned. From the colonial era has come the equation of school success with examination success, and the shadow of Cambridge School Certificate and the New Zealand University Entrance still hangs over the Pacific scene like a post-colonial smog, so it seems that the only way that people can be fairly selected for higher education at a totally new institution like the University of the South Pacific is by means of examination systems. No other system of selection has ever been contemplated. But other systems could be instituted; for instance, each village or island community could nominate its own students for higher education, teacher training and such on a quota basis and according to national personnel needs. The immediate objection to such a scheme would be that such a method would consolidate the position of the élite and thus be unfair—and surely an examination system avoids that. But does it? Those who come through to higher education, even under an examination system, are often the children of families of wealth and status. They have often had more educational opportunity anyway. Nepotism in educational selection cannot always be avoided.

The examination system subjects students and schools to two highly undesirable experiences. One is an experience of failure for many which is quite disproportionate to their real progress in learning and the second is its effect upon schools and teaching styles. Papua New Guinea tried to devise and use psychometric tests rather than educational exams of the usual kind(86). This was a bold step but children then were selected into an educational system that went right on being dominated by examining. Ultimately, systems that rely on continuous assessment of what children know and which develop the professional responsibility and skill of teachers to make selection recommendations may supplant the crudity of exams.

How do Polynesian children handle failure? Their background socialisation provides for them a clear answer. You withdraw from, you isolate yourself from, that which causes the failure. It is as simple as that. There is no great mystery about why it is that Polynesian students turn off from schools and present the dropout phenomenon that Gallimore and associates describe for Hawaii and Bobillier notes in New Zealand(17, 38). Polynesian children do not see any reason to persist in something if failure is the certain expectation. Why start on the route which clearly leads to it? There is a realism and a maturity about this sort of judgment that schools seem unable to handle. And so long as the schools continue to be examination oriented with as great or greater a prospect of failure as of success a great many students will declare them irrelevant to their lives in spite of parental injunctions and community pressures. As places to be they are too punishing to be tolerated.

We have heard endless discussion around the Pacific of the difficulties encountered in instituting national evaluation systems and we have been too timid to ask why anybody considers them worthwhile. The reason people give for them is that where educational resources are limited not all can have all the education they (or their parents) want. Well, we understand that well enough. But there seems something rather curious about the present situation where in New Zealand a developed (or overdeveloped) education system is fighting to get rid of national examinations while many Pacific countries are struggling to set up their own.

There is something inherently wrong and very disturbing about the argument that the tertiary education system of the Pacific will be somehow better off when it sets up its own entrance board and entrance examination to replace the New Zealand or British system. Doubtless, Pacific countries could design an examination system for entrance to university more relevant to the Pacific scene than New Zealand School Certificate or University Entrance, and now that a South Pacific assessment board has been established they will. But the criteria of who shall be future leaders in the political, commercial and social life of the Pacific may be limited simply to those of school attainment and knowledge. There may be good reason to have country or ethnic quotas at the university and to allow the status and social development needs of particular island groups to play some part in the determination of who gets further education. To achieve that sort of objective would require some rather hardline political talk to such bodies as the New Zealand University Entrance Board, which continues to exercise a modern version of colonial power and dominance over some parts, at least, of the Pacific and some hard reassessment of what shall constitute success at university. The same could be said, in even stronger terms, about the domination of Paris over education at all levels in French Polynesia.

In the past the examination issue has consolidated the conservative influence of colonial teaching styles further perpetuated through teacher training. One notable New Zealand educator, Clarence Beeby, has presented the argument that an education system evolves along a continuum dominated at the beginning by the task of achieving basic and universal literacy and extending to liberal education for a free society at the other end of the scale. Thus he sees the emphasis on monitoring, rote learning and basic skills in teacher dominated classroom systems in many developing countries as being the evolutionary equivalent of the early mass educational schools of the industrial revolution in the West, the so called 'dame schools'(10). Beeby saw the present level of educational development in the Pacific as extending well beyond this but still not yet ready for the modern style of so-called progressive teaching with its use of project and discovery methods, individualised instruction and self-generated activities and curricula (which is regarded as the best educational practice in a developed country like New Zealand).

We think the time has passed when Pacific people will accept this type of 'second best' argument from anyone. Whatever the history of Western education may have been, like any other history it has largely been a matter of unenlightened stumbling from one coping situation to another in a context where the community basis of culture has either been unclear or declared irrelevant. The 'dame school' was just a bad model that happened to be adopted at a time of scarce public resources because the economy was dominated by the greed of capitalists. There is certainly no need for the Pacific to continue to adopt, imitate or repeat that error, nor to rush to accept each innovative idea in education that happens to come along.

Over the last ten years the island locations which have managed a clear break to independence have been better able to develop their own educational style, Western Samoa being the most dramatic illustration. When one looks outside Polynesia the development of education in Papua New Guinea has proceeded rapidly and sensitively to meet the particular problems of that community of cultures(93). In other places such as American Samoa or the Cooks no one much seems to want local autonomy but there is still a strong cultural consciousness that local people want to see expressed in education, especially in language arts and social studies.

Colonial domination remains so strong and powerful in these places and in French Polynesia that the education system is likely to continue on a mainland metropolitan model there for some time yet. In the metropolitan centres of Hawaii, New Zealand and the US mainland Polynesian children must make their way as best they can within a system ill adapted to their dominant socialisation patterns and unlikely to be responsive to their cultural needs except in token ways. In such places it may now be time to urge the ethnic communities themselves to set up their own ancillary schools as the Chinese have done in many places or the Jews over most of their history.

The predominant effect of colonialism has been to emphasise a teaching style in which success has been related to individual achievements and evaluated by criteria that have little to do with being a good member of the village or other community.

Ted and Nancy Graves have contrasted learning styles in wholly European, ethnically mixed and entirely Polynesian classroom settings and have noted that Polynesian children like to work in integrated groups where they can experience contributory effort and thus gain satisfactions of social solidarity from cooperation(44). They call this style 'inclusive', by which they mean that Polynesian children prefer to act in ways that include other children in the activity as compared with European children whose preferred style is to exclude others and get on with the job. David Thomas, using an experimental technique in which children could act either competitively or cooperatively, found that Cook Island and rural Maori children were more cooperative than either urban Maori or Pakeha children(109). In later research he compared three groups of island children: Cook Islands, Samoan and Fijian, and found that the Cook Islanders were not only the least cooperative of the three groups studied, but that they were significantly more competitive in orientation than the Cook Island children he had previously studied(110). He explains this in terms of rapid social change and the role of the school which he sees as pushing the children towards individualistic and maladaptive Western competitive styles. The competitive style is a sort of survival requirement for success by Western criteria. Its costs are inefficiency and stress.

This research style and the leads which it opens up are of great interest but we return to one of our persistent themes, namely that Polynesians compete for Polynesian goals within a setting of cooperation. It is too simple a view to perpetuate the myth of happy cooperative Polynesians because any Polynesian will tell you just how darned uncooperative his or her family, community or kin can be from time to time. The status consciousness of Polynesian systems is itself fair evidence of (and explanation for) competitiveness in ordinary Polynesian life. There are elements in what both the Graves and David Thomas are saying which could indicate ways in which both learning style and teaching style may be more effective in the school setting, but in our experience these are just elements of good teaching everywhere. It is clearly maladaptive anywhere to maximise competitive individualistic learning, and the fostering of inter-group competition or rivalry could be as damaging as too much emphasis on individual achievement. The clue to seeing all this in perspective is to realise and appreciate that the proper functioning of Polynesian social systems requires that the individual be always seen in the context of the community or other social group. In the jargon of perceptual psychology, the individual is 'figure'-seen against the background of community. But sometimes the figure-ground relationship is reversed and the community becomes the figure, the dominant matter of concern, against which the individual must melt into the background. Thus, in their socialisation, Polynesians are learning in the context of family and community when to make such reversals, when to stand out, and when to stand back, when to go it alone and when to seek the help of their peers. The wise teacher, recognising this, will seek to make the classroom a model of these same social processes.

This question of adapting teaching styles to island settings cannot be easily dismissed by emphasising the use by individual teachers of a few pedagogic tricks such as introducing more group methods, using peer tutoring techniques, allocating group rewards, valuable though these are. The school as a whole must be seen as a community and as an entire social system and high schools particularly must be allowed to develop and operate a community authority system. By not generating respect or earning it they are in fact teaching disrespect. There have already been experiments in New Zealand with what has been called the *whanau* system in which large high schools are broken into small units. Autonomous in terms of buildings and each operating in an organisation of the teaching tasks which are regulated by the students and teachers of that *whanau* as a community group(53).

High school teachers should remember that their student population is composed of people who, in traditional tribal terms are already adults, albeit young adults, and that in their own context they would be expected to develop the qualities and attributes of community responsibility that traditionally applied and may still apply. If the community context outside the school has been so destroyed that this is no longer true the school cannot be blamed for that. But it can provide, in such a circumstance and for a time, a substitute community for the young person. The high school must deal with people who are sexually mature, know it and do not see any reason to hide the fact, who probably smoke and drink, who certainly want to dance and who will easily develop a hunger to learn the cultural knowledge that they need in order to be able to assume proper status in their own community. So these young adults need access to the status and respect languages, to the arts and skills of oratory, to traditional chant, to the history, myth and tradition which make these things meaningful. If they cannot get these inside schools they should have access to them outside. And they also need many opportunities to practice their skills in such areas and to reinterpret them in modern terms through creative writing, art, in the construction of new songs and other dramatic expression.

They also need the opportunity to understand the background of their local political situation all the way from what is happening in family and village to the national politics of the Pacific basin. There remains in most places a touchiness about approaching these matters in the context of the school. Hardly any of it penetrates the membrane that separates school from environment. This further perpetuates the isolation of the school from the community which surrounds it. Race relations, inter-ethnic misunderstandings, the background of trade and treaties, of the South Pacific Commission, the South Pacific Economic Commission and the Pacific Forum are the route to informed citizenhood, not optional extras.

Such a gap or barrier between school and community should never have been allowed to develop in the context of Pacific education and for the future one target for development could be to increase the involvement of the school in the community by such techniques as declaring public work days, providing regular entertainment on school premises, by involving elders to act as instructors and by using any other device or opportunity that may occur in any locality to integrate school and community.

In Papua New Guinea and in the islands of Palau oral history projects have directly involved high school students in the recording and transcribing of their own cultural records(93). The school should always be ready to down tools and get involved in what the community needs when there is community work to be done of any kind.

Back in the thirties the widening gap between school and community was noted with concern by those who attended the University of Hawaii Seminar Conference on Education in Pacific Countries but the solution then discussed was characteristically part of Western education, namely how to encourage Parent Teacher Associations to become effective(56). But here is what the PTA was seen to be: a small enclave of representatives (not the whole community itself) who meet from time to time (not invited to be continual advisers) to assist the headmaster and teachers (not the whole community of school plus people), to make the work of the headmaster and staff easier (when in fact to work effectively they should be making it more difficult). By continuously and insistently presenting the challenges of what the people want the school to do, not only for the children but also for the community, a PTA could be the innovative link telling the school what it needs to be doing. In every Pacific country, in every school, the opportunity exists in the present buildings, staff, and equipment for the total education of everybody in all things, traditional, modern, vocational, recreational, for men and for women. The concept of community schools, in this sense, has scarcely begun to be explored. School and community can, and should, develop together. All too often the school must become more and more competent while the community falls apart. Schools should be helping to build new communities, to maintain old ones and should always be answerable to them.

There is another peculiarity of the school as an institution. As an outgrowth of humanitarian concern for the young in Europe after the industrial revolution the school was designed to keep children out of the labour force where they were likely to be exploited as cheap labour to the detriment of their health and welfare. Therefore, school became children's work, a way of occupying the time of pupils in a peculiar kind of non-productive labour.

The Polynesian life-style provided, and in many places still provides, many useful ways in which children work for the sustenance of their own community. But when school takes precedence over such activities, the integration of the growing child into the economic life of the village is broken and then must be re-established after the child has left school. This often leads to difficulties. There is no reason in the wide Pacific why this should be so or why the timetables of individual schools on particular islands should all be the same by day, by week, or by year, since in this way problems such as truancy are generated. Truancy is a problem created by educational systems, not by children or parents or the intrusion of foreign influences or ideas into the minds of the young. The problem can be removed by changing the system so that the needs of children, parents and communities have the precedence which belongs to them. No one plays truant from the movie house, pool room or surfing beach in order to get to school—it's always the other way around. Schools are not sufficiently attractive. Headmasters may protest that they are not competing in the entertainment business, and they are not, but perhaps they should be.

The location for which we have most information on matters of this kind is Hawaii where McDonald and Gallimore and Sloggett put into operation deliberate programmes to overcome such problems(69, 107). They used techniques derived from the theory of behaviour modification. They were dealing with non-achievers who were likely to become drop-outs, unemployed and a nuisance around the place. They encouraged school attendance by giving group points and each group set their own goals and their own rewards for reaching those goals. The youths were not even required to attend all the school day; the emphasis was on basic skills. Each individual's progress was carefully assessed and he and the group were informed of it; the group was rewarded for each individual's efforts. The project was dramatically successful for the target pupils; but it should be remembered that this was clearly a remedial programme to salvage a small group of potential derelicts, victims of the Honolulu drug environment and candidates for crime. When the education system has produced problems of this kind, something special has to be done for them, but the problem need never have arisen had the school been seen to be part of the local community and responded to the large number of Hawaiian students on its rolls in appropriate ways.

In another case Oliver, working in Suva with shoe shine boys, used similar techniques (though on an individual basis) also with quite spectacular success(84). Petty crime among the kids dropped away entirely and they began to work at cash jobs, occasional at first but then more often. They also got points for attending English language classes. In this way the boys showed how to combat rising rates of juvenile crime, a problem of some concern in Fiji(22). Perhaps in all such cases some cross-over programme between school and outside work could go far to alleviate problems. Young people need to go on learning but they also often need cash and the more adult status of working.

Whenever the argument of increased community relevance is presented, someone is sure to point out such suggestions fly in the face of modernisation, that people are leaving villages, no longer live in communities and that there is no point in advocating a 'back to the mat' policy. This argument is mostly about words, not realities. If you want computer programmers, they can be trained in three months even if the training must take place off island. A modern economy does require such specialists as lawyers, accountants, veterinary surgeons, doctors, motor mechanics—but only in very small numbers and the education system as a whole should not be distorted merely to produce a few specialists. If one asks what a modern education might comprise for people generally in the islands of Polynesia, the particular answers will come out in different patterns but will generally list such basic skills as literacy, numeracy, enough knowledge to take an intelligent interest in current affairs and to participate in democratic and political processes, and to be a good family and community member. All these objectives can be achieved within a community school setting and, we would argue, can be better done this way, because that is where children growing up will continue to learn all the additional things that schools cannot possibly teach them about being a good Tongan, or being a good Pukapukan. Furthermore, even in cities, Polynesians resolutely try to reorganise a community life like the one they know back home.

There is no doubt that in some locations, for example American Samoa, the Tokelaus and the Cook Islands, a larger proportion of young people are destined to migrate and this argument has certainly been used in places like American Samoa to support the continued use of expatriate teachers and to justify a US oriented curriculum. We will discuss this in more detail in the next chapter. No education system can realistically be expected to teach all the requirements of living somewhere else which can mostly be learnt after migration. Within the metropolitan countries there is from time to time public outcry about the lack of preparation of Polynesian migrants and there is even diplomatic pressure on island governments to set up their own pre-migration training schemes. In our view this is a problem for the host country which, since it is going to employ the labour of these people, should accept the obligation to provide the supports for them to live adequately in the new environment or better still, assist the resident migrant population to look after its own in the new setting which in some locations both Tongan and Samoan groups are certainly doing for some. Recently discussions have been held via a communications satellite in which island leaders in various mainland US localities and in Hawaii discussed problems of migrant adaption and urban community development.

True Polynesian identity develops only in a context of place and folk and local tradition. There is an intellectualised kind of identity one may acquire by book learning or by study or through secondary socialisation but it's not the same thing. When Maori people or any other person can find no other way back to an ethnic identity that route must do. Such an identity can be a strong thing in its own right but it is different because without community around it is hard to see how the essence of Polynesian style can be expressed. All too easily an individual may become not really a Polynesian at all but a culturally detached international person at best, at worst forever deprived of personal security, a culturally dispossessed waif, stray or derelict, owing allegiance to no code or creed or community, washing from one Pacific port to another, or submerged in some wider population.

The loneliness and separation from locality that one reads of in statements such as the novels and stories of Albert Wendt or Witi Ihimaera are not alienation in the Western sense, but something else. For all the pain they express we see in them a strong developmental message: it may not be comfortable to long for one's own home, village and background, but at least one knows where one belongs and what it is that one longs for, what one lacks and where and how to find it. It is just that circumstances do not fit or one is not prepared to pay the social and personal costs involved in returning home. But relatives always welcome the homecomer. So great are the satisfactions of place and folk which Polynesians are generally able to enjoy as they grow up in such settings that they will rarely be comfortable somewhere else unless they recreate their cultural version of the Polynesian way wherever they are. We know of Maoris who have done so in Sydney, of Samoans who have done so in Tokoroa, of Cook Islanders in Porirua, American Samoans in Hawaii, Kapingamairangians in Ponape, who are nonetheless still members of their own culture. The Polynesian migration goes on.

CHAPTER *13*

At Home and Abroad

'I feel that Polynesians wishing to migrate to other countries ought to be prepared in their respective home islands for the migration. I believe that it is only while they are still in their familiar settings that Polynesians can find out all that they should know about a new country without any reservation. And should they encounter difficulties, there are so many people they can turn to for advice. On the other hand, if they are already in an alien environment, especially one where community living is non-existent then the thought of even asking for assistance won't ever be entertained by the migrant.'

'If New Zealand or the United States accepts the migrant Polynesian then they should assist them to adjust. For too long the metropolitan countries have utilised labour forces which did not cost them a cent to breed and nurture to adulthood. They should at least have the decency to improve their welfare as they are a labour force obtained very cheaply.'

'Most people whom I've talked with when they've come back to Tonga have complained about the working conditions and the time allocated for work. They had to wake up at 5 am so they can catch the bus to work. They stayed there and came back home almost at sunset. Time is the boss, they said. At home they can go to their plantation at any time and come back home when they want to.'

'Life in the factory is so boring. You have nobody to talk to except at smoko-time. At home they mostly organise themselves in a group and always work together.'

'Money is easy to get in New Zealand, but even easier to spend. However, the need for a higher standard of living outweighs the anti-social experiences at work.'

'At first, the return home is the main objective, then as the years go by and the immigrants become established, the thoughts of home fade until finally, with marriage and children, this is completely forgotten.'

'The reluctance to return home stems from the lack of opportunity for financial earning to support oneself, let alone the family, at home. There is also a reluctance to return to the Samoan way (Faa Samoa) under the matai system where one no longer has the freedom to do what one likes, as one did in New Zealand.'

'A revival of Samoan curricula in the Samoan language more than ten years ago (1966) has changed our outlook tremendously. We now feel that not only do we have the desire to keep the Faa–Samoa, but we have been provided with the language tools to do this, and these are very powerful tools indeed.'

'Young people at home in Tonga associate liquor with aggressiveness. For example, if I get angry with another young man I would drink liquor then challenge him. Perhaps as they go overseas they take this idea with them.'

'I have seen Fijians in Brisbane getting together at Christmas and New Year and recreating the Fiji-style celebrations there. They were nostalgic occasions, as though it was just like being home. The songs and language and even the food were as close to home as one can get at that distance. However, work and distance makes these occasions rare.'

'One thing I did notice that Fijians seem very much closer overseas. I've noticed that in Hawaii, Brisbane and Auckland. People one wouldn't normally have anything to do with at home suddenly become a great big family overseas even without a church organisation. I also found at the East West Center that Polynesians, Fijians included, just drew naturally together. There seems to be a "kin" feeling that brought us together.'

Continuing migration has been and will continue to be an abiding feature of Polynesian life. Already it has been estimated that for every American Samoan living at home on the islands, there are two living somewhere else. The Tokelauan population in New Zealand exceeds that of the home island and some 18 000 Western Samoans are living in New Zealand. There are as many Cook Islanders there as on-island and twice as many Niueans. In addition, inter-island migration is quite profound as in the Tongan community in Pago Pago, the Kapingamarangi village in Ponape, settlements of almost every Polynesian kind in Hawaii, the Banabans in Rambi island in Fiji or the way Rotumans are found almost everywhere(251). The scope of this may be greater now than in the past but islanders have always tolerated one another and been ready to make provision for migrants and castaways.

If one wants a higher income than the island can provide, then nowadays migration is the means to attain it. Among young island people that one might speak to almost anywhere, there is an intense interest in travel. This is no way different from the desire of non-Polynesian New Zealanders to go to Australia, England or the East. The desire to travel knows no ethnic boundaries. From studies of Samoans who sought long-term migration to New Zealand, we have a little information about their motives(89). Higher wages, helping the family at home, joining relatives and further education were the major reasons stated, but the large majority could not state any reason at all: they just came. That might seem pretty aimless, but spending some time off-island has become part of the dream that young people in Polynesia share. They will do it if they can and they do not seem to need other reasons. Considerable sums of money flow back to the homelands from migrants elsewhere. Some local economies would be in trouble without this.

From the Samoan study, and we suspect more generally, those who migrate expect one day to return; maybe they will but the permanent expatriate numbers continue to increase. Expectations of temporary residence do not, however, prevent them from setting up more or less permanent community associations in cities in the Pacific rim: Auckland, Honolulu, San Francisco, Los Angeles. Pitt and McPherson have produced a very sympathetic account of the ways Samoans handle the tasks of life as a minority group in New Zealand cities(89). They stress the role of the *aiga* (extended family) in providing social security and support and their account definitely ties the Samoan experience overseas back to the village systems and social structures of the islands. They mention only briefly the unsympathetic attitudes of surrounding New Zealanders and they do not draw out the real distinction which is arising between the island-born and those who never knew the island home. They are optimistic that the generation which has been born here can successfully assimilate to, and assist in, a kind of community organisation modelled on that of the island homeland. But young Polynesians growing up in a metropolitan country are surrounded by the youth culture of that country which carries messages of a different cultural quality to those of Polynesian peer groups in island settings.

One serious area of concern is the disruption (sometimes complete destruction) of the responsiveness of young people to the status–authority systems in their new or old communities. In island homelands young people do not generally have access to liquor as readily as is the case in the metropolitan centres and if under its influence they become aggressive and engage in fighting there, family and community authority may be exercised over them so that they know very well the social consequences of behaving in an unruly manner. Indeed so sharply may they feel the shame of misconduct that adolescent suicide is a problem, these days, in both Samoas, in Tahiti and possibly elsewhere too. Not only is the release of aggression in a big city easier, and its consequences less obvious, but the city environment in itself may be more frustrating, thus inducing more aggression.

There are many sources of frustration. Some arise from poorly understanding the language around them or being themselves poorly understood. Some occur through misreading social cues so that slights and insults are seen where none exist or accurately reading them and resenting those which do indicate intended insult. Problems connected with housing, job, diet and having to survive long cold winters in a foreign place, not being able to afford all the good things that were expected, having to respond to family demands that do not apply to their Maori or Pakeha workmates, all these may become sources of anger. Problems of sexual access become enormously complex when you are outside your known folkways. And in much the same way where once you knew how and when to show anger and how much, the loss of folkways and contexts can lead to a disoriented acting out in inappropriate situations and ways. But greater than any other factor may be a perception that you and your group are regarded by the surrounding society as of low status, that you are seen by many as somewhat unwelcome visitors and that you are subject to laws in matters such as entry permits that do not apply to many of the people around you. Those who have and keep strong church affiliations find these to be not only of great comfort but also of great assistance in making adjustment to the new situation and the maintenance of contact with their kind. But again, the second generation, expatriate-born, have grown to maturity in an environment far more secular than that of their parents and as new people in the new land may reject the support of the old religion. Rugby and the pub may seem to bring more social satisfactions than church and the old culture did.

Two aspects of the migrant experience cause grave difficulties for almost everyone. The first is language and the second is adjustment to work. Though we have not discussed the matter earlier the question of which language or languages will best fit Pacific people for a modern future soon arises wherever either education or migration is under discussion. Where, as in American

Samoa, a large number of young people, perhaps the majority, are forced to live off-island because there is no living for them at home, there really is no question but that learning English is a vital part of the necessary equipment to understand the modern world and to move with freedom within it. There is no doubt that without basic facility in English, whether people live on-island or off-island, their experience and their freedom to move will be limited. English is the common language by which the cultures of the Pacific (with the exception of French Polynesia) are able to converse and so there is no realistic alternative but to maintain bilingual education.

The debate then turns on the question of whether Pacific education systems, indeed parents, should aim at true bilingualism right through the whole educational structure or whether there should just be a later concentration on English as a second language much in the same way as children in English speaking countries learn French or German.

True bilingualism arises in situations where both languages have equal status in the environment, where they are equally heard, equally prevalent. It is doubtful whether, without tremendous effort and expense, linguistic inequality can ever be reversed where, as in Hawaii or New Zealand English has taken over and the vernacular use of the native tongue declined. Some effort to do this has occurred in some places, Wales for example. All that this has demonstrated is that a national vernacular can be saved from extinction by giving major emphasis to it in schooling. The dominant language of the Welsh environment is still English, and all the effort that has gone into developing the Welsh language through schooling has saved the Welsh language from disappearing entirely but has not created a truly equal language environment. However, where there is something approaching linguistic equality, as in French Canada, it seems tragic that the emphasis on wholly French language schools is distorting the truly bilingual nature of children's experience.

In the New Zealand situation, while the number of native Maori speakers has been progressively falling, government, educational authorities and Maori leaders have sought to stage a revival in the school use of Maori. The children, however, are growing up in a predominantly English language world and at least until they are teenagers Maori has little more than novelty value for them, if that. We think this means for both Maori and non-Maori children that Maori must be a second language.

True bilingualism and knowing a second language are very different things. The techniques of language teaching are very different also. If in the New Zealand case a clear decision was made that Maori would be taught as a second language to children of intermediate school age and above, and effort and resources were concentrated on this, we might see more coherent and rapid progress in curriculum, in materials and in teaching methodology than has been the case. Similarly in most island Pacific locations teaching English as a second language is the clearest policy alternative. The children will hear some English in the ordinary environment so that they will have some background on which to develop English as a second language later. The time to begin is somewhere in the primary school—when depends on local circumstances. From what we have already said about school and community it is clear that the school should be teaching in the vernacular of the home. Later almost every child, as he or she grows to maturity, will need sufficient English to follow what is going on in the English language part of the environment. In some cases this is very little, but it will increasingly include the news of the world as well as the island background. English will be needed by all so both it *and* the local language need to be part of the school experience.

Adequate English is already a requirement of entry permits to New Zealand and the United States but it is our impression that in neither case is the requirement rigidly enforced. On migration, if English is not adequate for the minimal requirements of the new environment, the migrating individual is subjected to quite needless stress.

Who is to judge what is adequate? In our view that standard is best set by those who have been through this experience and not by some external official whose native language is English and whose standards may be unrealistically high. Furthermore, we know that island communities are beginning to conduct their own courses and classes in functional English in the metropolitan environment. The Auckland Pacific Islanders Educational Resource Centre offers classes both at the centre and in islanders' own homes.

The other severe migrant problem is accommodating to the work environment—and here many adjustments are necessary. Hours worked in the urban environment are longer, more sustained, and require regularity. The jobs are generally dull and repetitive, especially in industry, and are for the most part of low status.

One is expected to acquire skills in the job but often prior instruction is minimal. Frequently people will be required to work shifts, with disruption to their family relationships. Because in New Zealand an employer must guarantee work before a work permit can be granted, individuals are subject to pressure from their own group to be a good worker so that other members of the family can get similar guarantees. The individual in the New Zealand setting suddenly finds him or herself in a trade unionist environment, and therefore involved in stoppages, strikes and other industrial unrest which may be very disturbing if they do not understand what is going on or feel less loyalty to the trade union movement than to their family back on the island who depend on their wages. The nature of supervision on the job is very different from the rural village environment or even a port centre like Apia. And on top of all this, the individual is constantly at risk of being fired, which is a greater threat to an islander than to other workers. He or she will encounter stereotypes about islanders as employees which, whether or not they are true in general, may be felt to be unjust when applied to a particular person.

We doubt that much can be done about these problems in the island homeland prior to migration. And yet, because little is done about these things after migration, in many cases individuals suffer disillusionment and distress. The severity of the problem is increased where the metropolitan governments take the attitude that island migrants are in their country on sufferance and that though employers may value their labour, government policies often make them feel less than welcome, especially in times of economic recession. There is still much that is exploitative about the attitudes of metropolitan governments towards immigrant island labour whatever the protestations of intent to the contrary. While people go to the island as tourists on holiday, islanders come to the metropolitan cities as workers. There are worlds of difference separating these perspectives.

While the needs of migrants in respect of language and assistance with adjustment to working patterns is receiving some recognition from government agencies and from resident island populations, the difficulties which parents encounter in maintaining a Polynesian style of child rearing are scarcely recognised.

One of the unhappiest field research experiences we have had was among a group of Maori people, for the most part first-generation migrants into a small rural town(97). The parents in this situation lacked the environmental supports to raise their children in the manner in which they had been raised. They were surrounded by non-Maori families whom they saw as being ready to criticise. These Maori parents had lost faith in their own system, were busily trying to operate on what they thought was the Pakeha method of bringing up children and so were inordinately severe on the children over whom they exercised a great deal of vigilance. They mythologised the city, to which their youngsters went and where they often landed in trouble, as a demonic monster gobbling up their young.

The city does not provide many open spaces. In its environment there are many dangers. Unsupervised groups of children are often regarded with suspicion. The agencies of law are impersonal, bureaucratic; they make little allowance for cultural variations and rightly or wrongly are often accused of prejudiced discrimination in arresting and sentencing procedures. Houses are small and their uses are specified and governed by city ordinances. The social and economic supports of community are not always readily available, the money economy is total and people are subject to expensive, exploitative and sometimes predatory consumer influences such as insurance and encyclopaedia salespeople and those who tempt them into hire purchase agreements. There is often no surrounding world of adult aid in child rearing; health and hospital facilities are not always within reach, local remedies and health advice are not available.

Schools take away their child caretakers, operate on a different cultural system and inculcate values that are quite alien to the Polynesian lifestyle. Instead of the school being that nice little building we made in the village for our children, it is a large, seemingly crowded busy place whose teachers are strangers, within whose walls one may feel so hopelessly lost and alienated that one is struck dumb.

To counteract all this will require very positive and strong appreciation about those aspects of one's childrearing that one seeks to preserve, and sometimes firm insistance that organisations such as the school, the welfare agency, the police should try and see things from a Polynesian point of view. It is all too easy for the majority culture to say 'You're here now, you do it our way or you go home'. And that is not very helpful, equitable or just.

Confronted with a higher status authority such as a headmaster or the police it is not characteristic of Polynesians to be firmly insistant on their rights against his or her status. But it is their way to speak through someone of status who can present their point of view and this should be done wherever necessary.

If what we have said about urban living sounds totally negative and depressing, we should balance this by saying that there is no doubt that Polynesians, in their own community and cultural groups, have tremendous fun in the city. Their dances, their sports meetings, their bazaars and other Church functions bring festivals back into their lives as well as or better than they could enjoy back on the island.

From our Maori research, we have observed that, given time, families can reassert their own socialisation patterns quite adequately in an urban environment(97). Many, of course, simply switch over to Pakeha methods of child rearing without even realising that this is happening. But not all. An extra pair of adult hands in the house can be provided by an aunt or uncle living with the family; some families, increasingly more, will want to limit their number of children in the interest of providing better care and more opportunities for them. Some schools, particularly where there are Polynesian teachers, go to great efforts to lay the foundations for Polynesian identity, even in language, allowing the uses of any or all of the Polynesian dialects quite freely. Some families link up with their youth clubs, church and other community support groups from their own culture so that they and their children may avoid the closeness and tightness of living in an isolated nuclear household. Many island families go to some lengths to see that the island homeland remains an active part of their children's consciousness. They sing about it, treasure its memories, speak often of the ardent desire to return home.

Slowly, there is growing a small body of creative writing by Polynesians in which young people may vicariously experience the Polynesian ordering of sentiments and forms of thought and expression. The role of the University of the South Pacific in stimulating and supporting this has been of great significance.

It is possible to reconstruct an urban variant of village feasting and food styles. Increasingly, music and dancing provide young people with the opportunity to participate in and to display something seen to be uniquely theirs. Even in European entertainments like rock bands and talent quests, Polynesians repeatedly lead the band and scoop the pool. This is a status actively respected at least by the young in both Polynesian and non-Polynesian cultures. Not only can children learn to demonstrate their own distinctive cultural background in these ways, but also they can very readily learn each other's and thus get real satisfaction from helping to develop the future common culture of Polynesia. A good multi-racial classroom can do wonders in this respect(37). When a teacher realises the cultural resources before him or her in the ordinary experience of the children a whole perspective of teaching opens(93).

Inevitably in metropolitan cities there is some homogenisation of the distinct life-styles going on. It is not uncommon to find a dance group who can readily produce their version of a New Zealand *haka*, or a *poi* dance, a Samoan *siva*, the Tahitian *tamure* or Hawaiian *hula*, plus any number of 'party' songs and ditties from half a dozen Polynesian traditions. The popular arts often pre-figure the future. Pan-Polynesia will not come by policy or persuasion but because people find things in common which they enjoy sharing. The South Pacific Festival of the Arts, held every two years, is doing much to stimulate a regional consciousness, more, probably, than the politics of the Pacific Forum.

Both the Maori and the Hawaiian experiences show how resilient Polynesian cultures are, for though subjected to every kind of destructive force save annihilation itself, the capacity to adapt, to incorporate, to include, to share and yet to remain distinctive has endured. Rather than become less, some cultural growth is now more vigorous than ever before. People have become comfortable in new surroundings. As suspicion and distrust die off under common need or through working together for common goals, ethnic tensions matter less. As people start learning how to use the new media of communication, radio and TV and little newspapers to speak to one another as well as to the wider world their cultural identities emerge. Always having been small, Pacific cultures easily think small and do the necessary things of cultural survival because there is nothing else to do.

CHAPTER *14*

Human Development in a Pacific Perspective

'Perhaps only a few Polynesians are conscious of the various themes that are raised in this book. Most Polynesians are proud of the fact that they are Polynesians, but what they are adopting does not seem to promote the Polynesian way of life.'

'Lack of praise from adults is typical in Samoa. I always think back to the pains of growing up when I recall the many thrashings received from older brothers, cousins, aunts and parents. Thinking back on all the disciplinary measures, there were times I suppose it was necessary when I consider the kind of mischief we were involved in as youngsters—in swimming, playing cricket or just growing up. All in all, I still have fond memories of an adventurous life when there were no adults around.'

'In Tonga we have a proverb that is commonly used and that is "Potopoto a niu mui" (clever young coconut). If a young person does something that is worthy of praise the old folks only say that he is too clever for his age. They don't praise him.'

In this chapter, we will try to draw together what seem to us to be the major cultural goals of socialisation in Polynesia, to look at Polynesian socialisation in terms of those few general principles which seem to have come through in the literature of child development and to draw attention to what seem to us to be some of the changes taking place or that possibly lie ahead in the development of the Polynesian pattern.

In this book we have attempted to take a cultural perspective, that is, we have placed what we think are the dominant features of Polynesian culture patterns at the forefront of our thinking and then we have tried to look at growing up in terms of these. Obviously, this is a very different approach to that of the usual child development text, where no particular cultural frame of reference exists. However, when developmental psychologists have managed to get outside their own cultural perspective they readily become aware of the limitations of the standard texts and approaches(60). Bronfenbrenner's comparative report on the role of peer groups in socialisation in Soviet Russia and the USA was greeted with widespread interest and approval on the child development scene even though cross-cultural studies had been making the same point for thirty years, unheeded(19). For the most part anthropologists made their points for the culture they were studying with the exception, always the notable exception, of Margaret Mead.

In the field of child development one generally must proceed with the greatest of caution, for its theories or principles may be really nothing more than studies of one particular culture's pattern of socialisation. As we said at the beginning, if child development research were dominated by researchers, samples, problems and procedures from Samoa rather than the USA, the text books would look very different. For example, the copious writings of Jean Piaget and the flood of studies that have flowed from them are reported in texts of child development as though the stages and milestones which Piaget's theory set up are universal, unchangeable and established. This is just not so. They are Western, and there is sufficient cross-cultural evidence of this fact to seriously question their universal application to all cultures(82). This is why we do not use or advocate Piagetian theory in our writings. We are suspicious that it may have more to do with the resurgence of structuralism as a modern intellectual fashion in Europe than with how you learn to respect your *matai*.

The usual way in which people approach the sorts of topics we have been discussing in this book is to stack up the literature of child development and look through it to see how a particular culture appears in terms of it. Thus Erikson starts with a theory about identity and its development and then looks at, for example, the Yurok, in terms of it(32).

We have reversed this process because we believe that socialisation is not conducted in terms of the literature of child development but in terms of cultural goals. Adults everywhere want their children to grow up not simply to be good human beings in universal terms but to be good people in their own cultural terms. This means that they want their children to act in particular ways, to exhibit particular qualities of character, to share common values with their parents and other adults in their communities. The problem that has arisen in taking our approach is that in any culture central values are mostly unstated. It is hard to get at them. Desired character is so taken for granted that people can only find very general and abstract ways of expressing it. People speak of honesty, integrity and so on but these only become meaningful in a specified and defined context. So we have been forced to go to the writings chiefly of anthropologists—outsiders to the cultures, as we ourselves are—who have been able to use their outside viewpoint to see what it is that Polynesians do that makes them different from other cultural groups. The risk in this is that, being outsiders, they and we may, from a Polynesian point of view, not get things quite right. We hope that there will be copious discussion and criticism of this book by Polynesians for in that process the cultural goals will be made more clear. This is even more important because these goals are being eroded by the intrusion of outside cultures and their attainment made more difficult by uncritical acceptance of external institutions such as the school. It is with some apprehension, therefore, that we come to summarise the nature of Polynesian cultural goals.

Our temerity is increased by the fact that in the past Western observers have so often seen Polynesia in such strange terms. The Pacific was explored at a time when Western philosophy had gone on a binge of high romanticism and so Polynesians were characterised as noble savages living in a state of primitive innocence. The genteel and often aristocratic scholars of the Royal Society seemed to rediscover in Polynesia the full glory, that was fading in Europe, of aristocratic status systems. They read Polynesian social structure as though it were some more perfect pre-industrial form of the status and privilege systems of the European past now drifting into decline, slipping away, fading. There were any number of scholar-gentlemen who were delighted to find an interpretation of religion and myth that reminded them of the classic cultures of Greece and Rome—as though Tangaroa had but recently descended from Mt Olympus. Polynesian warfare was seen as gentlemanly jousting. Bits that did not fit this picture, like cannibalism and infanticide, were conveniently overlooked or dismissed as an occasional aberration or degeneration from some noble Polynesian culture, pure in the past but now corrupt. The erotic quality of love songs and such Polynesian traits as the personification of the land in terms of female anatomy were prudishly suppressed. Polynesians were reclothed in the purer material vestments of Christianity and the Polynesian mind was overlaid in the same way.

Where it was inappropriate or simply wrong this idealisation can now be put behind us. But it was not all wrong. It is certainly true that Polynesia constitutes one of the high cultural traditions of the world, one of the peaks of humankind's continuous attempts to invent civilisation for itself. Living in comparative affluence its cultures had developed a variety of specialists, a complex social structure, a rich poetic tradition incorporating myth and expressed in song and oratory, and binding it all together a metaphysical depth that gave philosophic substance and a sustaining world view. These perspectives carried people beyond merely coping with the day-to-day requirements of living and they contained more or less conscious and explicit moral and religious statements. Whereas many non-Western cultures develop the life of the mind and the life of the soul largely in terms of magic and natural religion, the religious systems of Polynesia were backed by a cosmology and a sense of human destiny which made cultural goals more explicit. Magic there was, for there is perhaps a basic human need for it, but beyond and above it was an oral tradition that valued wisdom rather than hocus pocus.

Years ago Ruth Benedict postulated two major cultural orientations which she proposed might have some validity as a typology(11). Apollonian cultures were those which emphasised restraint, forbearance and the stoic virtues. Dionysian cultures, on the other hand, made a place for the ecstatic experience, valued immediate gratification and hedonistic enjoyment. When one comes to look at Polynesia in these terms, the system does not work because both things would be true. Polynesian warfare and politics were certainly in the tradition of Apollo but the love poetry, the feasting, the celebrations were as Dionysian as any Grecian wine festival. Robert Redfield puzzled over the inconsistencies between his account of the Mexican community of Tepoztlan and that of Oscar Lewis, and came to the major realisation that little communities often contain patterns which, on the face of things, seem contradictory though in practice do not seem so to their inhabitants(90, 63). Indeed, the 'work' of culture, he thought, might be to reconcile such inconsistencies (which does not mean to remove them). Tepoztlan seemed to Redfield a warm supportive community of happy festive people; to Lewis it seemed anxiety-ridden and riddled with distrust and vigilance. Could both be true? Yes, said Redfield, it depends on how you look at it: there is a cultural this and a cultural that.

We think this idea most useful in relation to some of the apparent contradictions of the Polynesian style. For example, we have mentioned the social obligations of the chief; the greater the status of such a person, the more bound he or she was to conceptions of community service. The greater the apparent emphasis on male status, the greater is the balancing role of women. Even in the mythologies the actions of a culture hero like Maui, who breaks all the rules, gives a role prescription or model for rule breaking. How can you have a rule that rules may be broken? While the greatest conservative emphasis was placed on the accuracy of genealogies or traditional chant, the body of tradition and myth has changed greatly over recent time, so that there is at least as much importance placed on creative adaption as on cultural conservatism. As one old Maori man said to one of us, 'You are supposed to make it up'!

The facts of cultural survival in Polynesia seems to us to be the starting point for a discussion of the nature of Polynesian cultural goals. Survival has been the dramatic fact of the voyaging history of Polynesia through space and time. For this to have been so successful there must have been, and were, cultural mechanisms that profoundly respected such human capacities as learning, valuing individual differences, giving individuals license to try new ways. We think that at core Polynesia has a this and a that about almost everything.

So the genius of Polynesian survival has been that its individuals were not required to make a simple choice between value extremes; they could toy with inconsistencies, take chances, break the old patterns, play with possibilities. And yet at the same time they had to do what they were told. These societies could value both the advantages of single-minded autocratic leadership (and make a place for *this*) and at the same time place a high priority on social consensus and democratic process (and make a place for *that*). They could respect the individual as having rights while at the same time emphasising community participation and respect for the wishes of the community. They could foster a competitive attitude and admire individual prowess while at the same time advocating a morality of cooperation. They could develop intricate systems of status and respect yet leave room for this to be challenged. And throughout all this custom and ritual operated to modulate all of these apparent contradictions into a social system that worked. Naturally, such a social system will not always work harmoniously, to say the very least. But this too is allowed for. For while social harmony is a goal, the capacity to speak out, to defend one's position, to go beyond simply agreeing with everybody was also valued. Logical opposites are not necessarily experientially intolerable. Having this, and that too, puts you beyond the conflict of choosing between impossibles.

These assertions concerning the nature of Polynesian culture may be met with some disbelief, especially from those who would see in such a system grave perils to an individual's mental health. But conflict may very well be a healthy human experience provided that, along with the conflict, there are also available ways of coping with it. Do you learn better to cope with conflict by avoiding or facing it? One of us, years ago, showed how in a small Maori community the balance between personal and social methods of coping with conflict was maintained, and Howard discusses the complexities of coping behaviour in a modern Hawaiian community(91, 52).

For people to learn to live in a culture whose alternatives are as complex as this required child rearing on quite a different model from the single parenting model which dominates the literature of child development. We are postulating here that there is a large quantity of complex social learning to be undertaken in order to achieve the cultural goals of socialisation. Throughout the growth of the child he or she needs to be taught to handle complexity and this may be done in a variety of ways. In the West, it is done by intensifying the long-term relationship with one major socialising person, the mother, then subjecting the child to the intense and complicated business of being psychologically weaned from her, then schooled, and finally subjecting child and parents to a long protracted process of gradual separation towards independence that takes decades to complete. The goal of socialisation is to produce an autonomous individual who can cope with any situation more or less on his or her own. The West has largely shed social mechanisms of supporting individuals in the face of complexities of living. You are on your own and have to have what psychologists call ego-strength to deal with the isolation. Polynesians would ask, simply, why?

In Polynesia, both the learning of complexity and handling conflicts has been mediated through multiple caretaking and peer socialisation. Through these mechanisms a child is never required to identify with and adopt the point of view of a single socialising individual but must match his or her behaviour to the persons in the environment. The right and possibility of leaving the environment and seeking another social situation more pleasant and satisfying is always present. This is an excellent way of dealing with conflict that can be used by children, adolescents and adults alike. Why beat your head against a wall when you can walk around it? The most delightful account of the Polynesian capacity to have your candy and eat it too is Ernest Beaglehole's description of The Candy Sucker's Art in Pukapuka which we reproduce in its entirety:

Pukapukan children have worked out to a fine art their ability to gain the utmost pleasure from sucking boiled candy. You and I probably put candy in our mouths and chew it so vigorously that it disappears almost before we realize we are eating it. Not so a Pukapuka child. A piece of candy is a treasure to be cherished and enjoyed at leisure. If by some sleight of hand you can hide it about your naked body and escape to solitude past the watchful eyes of companions only too eager to share your pleasure, you first turn the candy over and over in your hands admiring its colour and texture in sunlight and shadow. Your hands are by now well and truly sticky so you lick them over for the sweetness on them. Then you tentatively place the candy on your tongue, but not for long, because it must be made to last. You withdraw the candy and pass your tongue over the inside of your mouth so that it feels sweet everywhere. Then you lick your fingers again and perhaps rub the wet candy over your lips and chin. This is so that you may now poke out your tongue and thoroughly clean the stickiness from lips and chin. You continue placing the candy on your tongue and rubbing it over your fingers and licking your fingers afterwards until the candy has half disappeared. Then you hide it in your hair or in your ear for mid-morning refreshment later on.

It is only perhaps by the middle of the afternoon that a mishap causes you to swallow by mistake the minute portion which is all that remains of the early morning glory. And that is a regrettable nuisance because you had probably planned to finish the candy lying peacefully on your sleeping mat at bed time, hugging tight to yourself the secret pleasure of your enjoyment which your brothers and sisters half suspect yet do not share. And then in pleasant dreams of an island where the coral gravel has unaccountably changed to boiled candies and the fish of the sea have candy eyes and the trees have candy seeds, one more day of your busy childish life fades into forgetfulness.

Sometimes in a generous mood you share your candies with the gang. On a shady part of the beach each of your friends in turn is allowed to suck the candy for a second and then smear its wet sweetness over their hands and fingers. By the time it is your turn again, you have hands that are spotlessly clean. And so it goes until the candy has simply vanished with too much rubbing or else you decide to take the remainder home for your mother or favourite elders to enjoy as they sit cooling off on their special part of the beach. Young and old, from merest infant to hobbling great-grandparent, all alike appreciate the opportunity to suck to satiation. None, save perhaps the self-conscious manly young man, feels the slightest embarassment in bringing the white man eggs to be exchanged at three precious marbles of unbelievable sweetness for each water-tested egg.

I could never get used to the intense absorption of the Pukapukan child in the process of enjoying candy. It fascinated me beyond belief, this sensuous elaboration of the technique of securing with taste and touch and eye the utmost possible pleasure from the sweetness of easily dissolved flavoured sugar. But then, I suppose it was never my experience to be born and bred in an island community where nature was far from lavish with natural sweetenings. A few bananas grown by all three villages, minute amounts of papaia grown today by Yato, a little sugar cane grown in especially favourable soil by Loto village —that is all the Pukapuka can eat for natural sugars. Little wonder then that children and adults crave sugar, crave it best of all in the form of those small round colourful balls that are a long anodyne to the eager tongue and a continued joy to the anxious eye(5, pp. 163–165).

As a description of the subtle balancing of individual enjoyment maximised by group sharing it is magnificent, but doubtless Polynesian readers will be able to produce endless anecdotes of their own. In Polynesia you can always have your candy or your status, on your own if that is of any satisfaction to you, but sharing them, or anything else, increases the pleasure.

When we change focus to look at Polynesia in terms of general principles of child development we are a little perplexed because psychological writing in this area is so lacking in general principles and what there is undoubtedly has a heavy loading of Western cultural ideology. We are very concerned that Western text books of child development are being used in teacher and parent education in Pacific settings without this being appreciated. Their research basis is largely American, mainly white, and middle class values and practices are the norm against which the mores of other groups are tested and found wanting. In addition, because of the peculiar way in which the West has organised the science of human behaviour, much of the literature of child development reports research that is pursued as though only a single variable counts and the sociological (social) and anthropological (cultural) contexts of behaviour are largely ignored. Thus it comes as a great surprise to Michael Cole and associates that children change their use of mathematical concepts according to the situation in which they are being employed(24). Of course they do—everyone does.

Among the generalisations which the literature on child development has produced are some, however, which we feel we should discuss. Let us begin with the observations from the study by John and Beatrice Whiting and others of child training in six cultures. These authors show that where the mother has an economic role child training is likely to be shared with other adults(78). They also find that when there are many caretakers the load on any one of them is lighter and that mothers feel warmer towards their children. Many hands, so to speak, make not only light but also happy work.

Child development has placed great importance on the maternal role and in particular on the early attachment of the child to the mother so that this has assumed the status of a necessary and inevitable part of early development. Recently those who study animal behaviour have reinforced the emphasis on this so-called principle by generalising from animal studies the idea of bonding. This concept implies that the attachment of the child to the mother is instinctive, automatic in favourable circumstances and desirable. We doubt this. Human beings depend very little in their lives upon instinctive processes but rely instead upon learning, and if children become bonded in close attachment to their mothers it is because socialisation practices have been set up this way. Whether this is desirable or not depends entirely upon the social contexts that surround children and mothers. We certainly do not deny that bonding (close attachment) can occur, but on the basis of learning, not instinct, and bonding is therefore just an intense form of mother–child attachment. In Western societies this is emphasised and valued because there is no one else around for the child to depend on and (till recently) little else for the mother to do. It is simply nonsense to say that this degree of attachment is necessary and desirable in every culture and every case. Millions of human beings have grown up satisfactorily without it. Conversely, many mothers in Western suburbia have been driven to the edge of mental breakdown, and beyond, in trying to fulfil a notion of bonded motherhood that has been pressed upon them, be it by circumstances or by ill-informed so-called child experts(13). What have such experts to say of a New Guinea tribe where any lactating female will happily feed any hungry child or even a pig? The theory of maternal attachment is tied to the Western concept of individual ego and the ideology of rampant competitive individualism.

A great deal of recent child development research has been directed towards the exploration of the foundations of knowing in early experience. Even within the womb, a foetus sucks its fingers, drinks great quantities of liquid, responds to loud noises, flexes its muscles and has already begun on progressions of motor development which it will continue after birth, provided that those around it provide appropriate opportunity and experience. The early attention which children receive in Polynesia undoubtedly contributes to the development of these progressions, particularly in respect to motor development. We simply at this point lack any body of research on motor development in Polynesian groups. It is no accident, nor is it entirely a matter of genetic endowment, that Polynesians generally dance with grace and freedom and excel at sporting activities, for in these things they are probably receiving a good beginning which is followed through.

As the child grows, the literature of child development stresses the importance of a continuing, rich stimulating environment particularly in acquiring major skills like speaking or reading. Here the distributed childcare of Polynesia may not be serving its children quite so well, since children among themselves do not seem naturally and automatically to adopt or develop complex language structures. If children are to learn a language well, they need continual adult–child verbal interaction, careful but positive monitoring to eliminate language errors, copious and frequent models to copy. Whatever may be the case in Polynesia, we think that parents everywhere cannot talk too much to their children and probably do not talk enough.

Similarly peer play groups will not make much natural progression towards literacy or numeracy unless the people around them place this kind of experience before them. This can be done by means of peer socialisation, since older children can read to younger children, help them with homework, explain things generally if they are encouraged to do so and are praised when they do. But this is a new use of peer group structures. To feed into peer groups new ideas of how people can help one another is not difficult.

From our own research we know that Maori parents and adults make far less use of praise and reasoning than should be the case(100). We recognise that in Polynesian socialisation parents and adults are apprehensive that children should not become 'big headed', that is, assume above their status and act in precocious and conceited ways. That is a reasonable cultural concern, but if there is one conclusion in the literature that we can firmly endorse as being human and universal it is that if you want to increase the frequency of desirable behaviour reward it when it occurs. In Polynesia, to be noticed by a high status person is a powerful reward. To have one's behaviour appreciated by a collection of people is another. There is nothing culturally incompatible with the use of praise to encourage better behaviour in children if parents make a point of finding something to commend in each child's behaviour. In that way no one child will become swollen headed but all will gain in self esteem. Older children can be encouraged to apply the same principles to younger children and groups of children who are behaving well deserve to have that fact noticed and rewarded by a little gentle praise.

Children learn most when they are rewarded. Punishment certainly stops behaviour; but unless it is followed by some indication of the right or preferred behaviour it does little else. Because young children will avoid punishment if they can they also learn to avoid the presence of the person who punishes. We think that the readiness of Polynesian parents to punish children is one of the major ways by which children learn to prefer the company of those closer to their own age(97). But it is not necessary to punish children in order for them to interact away with their mates.

Punishment is very freely used by Polynesian parents. Our students commented on it and wherever we have been we have seen it all around us.

There are two problems that arise from the free use of punishment. Children who have learned that adults are potential punishers may generalise from the particular punisher to other adults, such as school teachers, and develop negative attitudes towards adults in general. The second observation we must make is that punishment develops aggression. Parents who are demoralised and are receiving a lot of environmental punishment themselves are more likely to punish their children who then take out their hostility wherever they can. To direct it towards the punisher leads to more punishment, so you learn not to do that! To attack an age mate, your physical equal, is also a bit dangerous so you are likely to take out your aggression on someone younger or weaker. And if you are then punished for that too, you will have to resort to more devious psychological strategies, more anti-social and even criminal activities such as setting fire to the school or other acts of vandalism. Such acts are always hostile against adults and authority; they always indicate that these are seen by the child to be punishers, and in fact they often are.

In the literature of child development infantile dependency has become a value—almost as though, without it, learning cannot take place. This is nonsense. Western societies have produced their own problems and conflicts concerning the balance between dependence and independence, delaying the assumption of full adult status until the end of the second decade of life. They have institutionalised a pattern in which children must engage in a struggle against parental authority and thus attain adult status only slowly and gradually throughout adolescence. Thus the high school as an institution is a poor training ground for adult responsibility since it treats young adults as children. In Polynesian cultures these problems and conflicts are lessened in the community, even if there has been a lessening of the ease and freedom which Margaret Mead wrote about in Samoa(75). But this is not so in the high school. The autonomy of young Polynesians is often astonishing when seen through Western eyes because Westerners are not used to the socialisation practices which lie behind it and have no appreciation of its cultural importance in developing the proper balance between individual and community. Given a European education system that assumes dependency and submissiveness on the part of children there are real conflicts for them between the environment of the school and the environment of the peer group.

Other problems in growing up arise where young people in urban settings become sexually active beyond the control of parents, community or anyone else, or roam in groups wherever they wish in the environment, or sleep where and with whom they please. Children are more likely to run into trouble with the law because they miss school, hang around street corners, indulge in shop lifting, but if their route to school does not lie through a city centre with all its temptations, the shop lifting and other nuisance behaviour is far less frequent. If schools became a home away from home and were open and available for youth activities throughout the afternoon and for part of the night, and at weekends as well, and provided the coffee bar, the disco, and craft, sporting and recreational activities that Polynesian children could easily organise for themselves, a bunk room even, youngsters would be less likely to get into trouble. There is no developmental reason why the Polynesian way of modulating independence against community dependency should change so long as there is a Polynesian community surrounding the process of socialisation. The nefarious aspect of urban independence is that the city is such a jungle, so dangerous, so impersonal, so lonely that young people can and do escape first into its mazeways and then become lost to their own culture entirely.

There remain great strengths in Polynesian ways of bringing up children and we will discuss these shortly. But there are also some modern day perils which need to be appreciated if they are to be avoided. Though we earlier cautioned against the use of the word rejection we have found examples of Polynesian parents who, in the absence of social supports for their child rearing, have become deeply rejective of their children especially where families are large and children close together. The strain on caretaking is too great and the family has become demoralised.

In another place we have examined in some detail why it is that both in New Zealand and in Hawaii more, far more Polynesian parents than should be the case, are involved in child abuse(99, 33). We are not merely speaking of harsh parenting practices or neglect but of physical brutalities. So far as we can tell from the literature we have surveyed this does not happen in the island homelands and did not in the past either. But now rates are six times higher for these migrant populations than for Europeans in the same environments. So why is this happening now and what should be done about it?

It is happening because the social protections against it, community vigilance, extended family parenting, alternative households all equally home, the comfort of and escape to the peer group just are not available in the city. The pattern is broken and not replaced by another. Strain, anxiety, unremitting presence of too many children, no help, no relief easily lead to anger and to attack. Alcohol use further reduces the threshold of abuse. All too often it is a route of escape that leads only to despair.

Maoris and Polynesians contributed 54 per cent of the children reported to the Social Welfare Department in 1967 in New Zealand as being not under proper control—though they constituted only 10 per cent of the population. More than 50 per cent of the children in state foster care there in 1977 were Polynesian. Clearly, foster care by the home community is no longer working adequately.

If, in the space of one generation these populations have shifted from a no-abuse to a high-abuse profile, what can be done about it? Since Western services have not come up with a corrective or preventative formula for such problems we would advocate the re-establishment of the Polynesian ways. There is no Western child rearing prescription, certain proof against child abuse, to which Polynesians could be shifted or in which they can be trained. Some have advocated self-help groups for child abusers that could work like Alcoholics Anonymous. The potential abuser needs help, that we recognise, but from whom? We doubt that a Polynesian parent in this kind of trouble will seek or accept help from a telephone call-in service, a Pakeha welfare worker or hospital medical social worker. But help from their own people, from inside their own culture, that could be acceptable. Communities can care for their own. Their children are all our children to be cared for as our own. Turn the problem back to the community.

But more than just community understanding and support is needed. We need to think of how the house of childhood can be raised again in new locations for new generations, how all the features of child training which we have discussed can be reconstructed, and become functional again in urban migrant locations. Can we design housing and plan cities so that multiple parenting can work? Can we modernise our ideas of mens' work and womens' work so that no one gets so trapped in unwelcome child care that the situation gets beyond tolerance? Can we not find ways to permit and encourage child minding by other children that is safe, in locations that are benign and not potentially lawless?

It is terribly, desperately, easy to shrug and say that such troubles have always accompanied migration and rapid social change. Anyone who repeats that sort of complacent hogwash needs to study just one serious case of child abuse and be shocked into the sanity of realising that *something* must be done. We think something can be done. Therefore something should be done. If the various migrant groups, Tongan, Samoan, Tokelauan, Niuean, Tahitian, Hawaiian, Rarotongan, Pukapukan, Maori get the chance and encouragement to do so they will recreate their folkways of child rearing as they will of church attending or any other part of their particular cultures.

Almost everywhere in the Pacific, child nutrition is causing some anxiety. When it is the cultural practice for adults to be fed first, children can find themselves left to scavenge, and their nutrition suffers. We know already that bottle feeding is a definite health hazard to babies and the sooner Polynesians get back to their traditional pattern of breast feeding the better. Parents need to be reminded that bread and tea is not enough for growing children and that, in particular, a daily quota of good protein is essential even in a seemingly affluent environment—whether in the island village or an urban situation. A society that really values healthy lively bright children will especially guarantee good nutrition to pregnant and nursing mothers. Traditionally there was a lot of attention to their diet; they were given special foods and whatever they craved in the interests of protecting their young, and they still need it. It is not yet widely recognised that when children, before they are born and in the first two years of life, do not receive adequate protein they suffer permanent and irreversible damage to their nervous systems. Their brain cells just do not develop and they suffer from what Lewin calls 'starved brains'(62). Then no amount of good feeding or good teaching can repair the damage.

Children anywhere cannot grow and learn unless they are healthy. Again, it is not generally realised how debilitating the minor stresses of childhood may be. Such infections as school sores, impetigo and sand sores may seem minor to parents but they are a breach of the body's defence system and with modern medication and health care there is no reason why children should suffer them. They are *not* minor and they *do* impede development. The incidence of middle ear infections with consequent damage to the mechanisms of hearing is a problem everywhere in Polynesia and in the cooler climates persistent bronchial infections must be avoided too. Teeth cause problems which can be a misery for the child and untreated fevers can have a devastating effect on children's growth for months if not years afterwards.

Certainly in New Zealand the services that would reduce these health problems are not reaching the people who need them most. We think that the basic problem is not one of health education

Human Development in a Pacific Perspective   161

but of the availability and delivery of health care. We suspect that this may be true elsewhere. Services set up by middle class people miss by a mile the less able, less wealthy, less culturally convergent people who are often badly in need of them(96).

In earlier times, the cultural style of relaxed socialisation with little pressure and no great demands of adult attentiveness could operate effectively because at initiation or later in life more intense socialisation experiences were available and were applied to ensure adequate performance of clearly defined cultural roles. Now this is not so and therefore it is necessary that parents play a more active and attentive role in the socialisation process. This need not necessarily be done by adopting the European model of intense training by one person, particularly by the mother. But it will require planning and thought to ensure that the two major supports of Polynesian socialisation, multiple caretaking and peer socialisation, will continue. We have seen many situations in New Zealand when this has proved to be possible, both for Maori and for Pacific Island people. But it cannot be done simply by attending to socialisation alone. You cannot have community socialisation without a community and there is no point in it unless the child becomes part of the community. So that to maintain Polynesian childhood one must maintain the Polynesian way of life. Children will best learn by participation rather than by instruction what its central messages are.

What are these? Who are we to say? We will not dodge the issue but we do not presume to have the whole answer. It seems to us that these must include that one maintains one's self esteem in the regard of the community and not beyond or apart from it; that others will give you status and respect when the time is right and when these have been earned, rather than by individual search and display; that one has the obligation to share with one's kinspeople and community; that one must accept community scrutiny of one's actions and the comment of others upon them; that just as, in time of trouble, one can turn for help and support to the group, so one must provide hospitality, support and material help when others turn to you. Can these things be planned for? Beyond the nuts and bolts of town planning, beyond the engineering, most of which we do know enough about, lie the prospects that cities can become like villages or small islands again where people can live responding to a folk around them who are their folk. This will not work for everybody but it does already for some and could for many more.

To live this way involves some personal costs, but what are the gains? The security of social support is one, lots of fun and pleasure, human rather than electronic entertainments another, sharing in the sadnesses of loss and trouble and death a third. And there are many many more. But most of all, uniquely, there is the strength of knowing that you step forward confidently in the long shadow cast by your ancestors, having an identity as one of a kind, of continuing in however small a way one of the great cultural traditions of the world's history.

References

1. Adorno, T.W., *The Authoritarian Personality*, Harper & Row, New York, 1950.
2. Aoyagi, M., 'Kinship Organisation and Behaviour in a Contemporary Tongan Village', *The Journal of the Polynesian Society*, Vol. 75, No. 2, 141–176, 1966.
3. Ausubel, D., *Maori Youth*, Price Milburn, Wellington, 1961.
4. Barnett, H.G., *Being a Palauan*, Holt, Rinehart & Winston, New York, 1960.
5. Beaglehole, E., *Islands of Danger*, Progressive Publishing Society, Wellington, 1944.
6. Beaglehole, E., *Social Change in the South Pacific*, George Allen & Unwin, London, 1957.
7. Beaglehole, E. & P., *Ethnology of Pukapuka*, Bishop Museum, Honolulu, 1938.
8. Beaglehole, E. & P., *Pangai Village in Tonga*, Polynesian Society, Wellington, 1941.
9. Beaglehole, E. & P., *Some Modern Maoris*, New Zealand Council for Educational Research, Wellington, 1946.
10. Beeby, C., *The Quality of Education in Developing Countries*, Harvard University Press, Mass., 1966.
11. Benedict, Ruth, *Patterns of Culture*, Mentor, Boston, 1934.
12. Best, E., *The Whare Kohanga (the 'Nest House') and Its Lore*. Dominion Museum Bulletin, No. 13, Wellington, 1929.
13. Bernard, J., *The Future of Marriage*, Bantam, New York, 1973.
14. Bernard, J., *The Future of Motherhood*, Dial Press, New York, 1974.
15. Biggs, B., *Maori Marriage*, Polynesian Society, Wellington, 1960.
16. Biggs, B., 'The Past Twenty Years in Polynesian Linguistics' in Highland, G.A., Force, R.W., Howard, A., Kelly, K., Sinoto, Y.H., (eds), *Polynesian Culture History*, Bishop Museum Press, Honolulu, 1967.
17. Bobillier, C., 'Truancy in New Zealand, A Survey of Eight Secondary Schools', *Delta*, 19, 57–62, November, 1976.
18. Bowlby, J., *Child Care and the Growth of Love*, Penguin, Harmondsworth, 1953.
19. Bronfenbrenner, U., *Two Worlds of Childhood*, Russell Sage Foundation, New York, 1970.

20. Burrows, E.G., *Western Polynesia*, University Book Shop Ltd., Dunedin, 1971.
21. Carroll, V. (ed.) *Adoption in Eastern Oceania*, University of Hawaii Press, Honolulu, 1970.
22. Chandra, S., 'Urban Delinquency in Fiji' in Harre, J. and Knapman, C., *Living in Town*, South Pacific Social Sciences Association, Suva, 1973.
23. Clay, M., 'Early Childhood and Cultural Diversity in New Zealand', *The Reading Teacher*, 333–342, January, 1976.
24. Cole, M., Gay, J., Glick, J.A. and Sharp, D.W., *The Cultural Context of Learning and Thinking*, Basic Books, New York, 1971.
25. Crocombe, R.G., *The New South Pacific*, Australian National University Press, Canberra, 1973.
26. Danielsson, B., *The Happy Island*, George Allen & Unwin, London, 1952.
27. Danielsson, B., *Work and Life on Raroia*, George Allen & Unwin, London, 1956.
28. Danielsson, B. & M.T., 'Polynesia's Third Sex: The Gay Life starts in the Kitchen', *Pacific Islands Monthly*, August, 1978.
29. De Vos, G.A., 'Achievement and Innovation in Culture and Personality' in Norbeck, E., Price-Williams, D., and McCord, W.M., (eds), *Personality: An Interdisciplinary Approach*, Holt, Rinehart & Winston, New York, 1968.
30. Dubois, C., *The People of Alor, A Social–Psychological Study of an East Indian Island*, University of Minnesota Press, Minneapolis, 1944.
31. Earle, M., *Rakau Children*, Victoria University, Wellington, 1958.
32. Erikson, E., *Childhood in Society*, Norton, New York, 1950.
33. Fergusson, D.M., Fleming, J. and O'Neill, D.P., *Child Abuse in New Zealand*, Government Printer, Wellington, 1972.
34. Firth, R., *We the Tikopia*, Allen and Unwin, London, 1936.
35. Frankovitch, M.K., *Child Rearing on Niue*, M.Soc.Sci. thesis, University of Waikato, 1974.
36. Frisbee, R., *The Book of Puka-Puka*, John Murray, London, 1930.
37. Gadd, B., *Cultural Difference in the Classroom*, Heinemann, Auckland, 1976.
38. Gallimore, R., Boggs, J.W. & Jordan, C., *Culture, Behavior and Education: A Study of Hawaiian–Americans*, Sage, Beverly Hills, 1974.
39. Gerrand, N., *The Book Programme*, Working Paper II, Centre for Maori Studies and Research, University of Waikato, 1975.
40. Geddes, W.R., *Deuba*. Polynesian Society Memoir, 22, Wellington, 1945.
41. Gladwin, T., *East Is a Big Bird*, Harvard University Press, Mass., 1970.
42. Goldman, I., 'The Evolution of Status Systems in Polynesia', in Wallace, A.F.C., *Men and Cultures*, University of Pennsylvania Press, Oxford, 1960.

43. Goldman, I., Status Rivalry and Cultural Evolution in Polynesia', *American Anthropologist*, Vol. 57, 680–697, 1955.
44. Graves, N.B. and T.D., *Inclusive Versus Exclusive Behaviour in New Zealand School Settings*, South Pacific Research Institute, 1973.
45. Griffen, V. et al., *Women's Role in Fiji*, South Pacific Social Sciences Association, Suva, 1975.
46. Hardy, M., 'Malnutrition in Young Children at Auckland', *New Zealand Medical Journal*, Vol. 75, No. 480, 291–295, 1972.
47. Hau'ofa Epeli, *Our Crowded Islands*, Institute of Pacific Studies, University of the South Pacific, Suva, Fiji, 1977.
48. Heuer, B., *Maori Women*, A.H. & A.W. Reed, Wellington, 1972.
49. Holmes, L.D., *Samoan Village*, Holt, Rinehart & Winston, New York, 1974.
50. Horner, M., 'Toward an Understanding of Achievement-Related Conflicts in Women', *Journal of Social Issues*, Vol. 28, No. 2, 157–175, 1972.
51. Howard, A., *Learning to Be Rotuman*, Columbia University Press, New York, 1970.
52. Howard, A., *Ain't No Big Thing: Coping Strategies in a Hawaiian–American Community*, The University Press of Hawaii, Honolulu, 1974.
53. Howarth, A.T.S., 'School Buildings, 1877–1977', *Education*, Vol. 26, No. 7, 7–17, 1977.
54. Jordan, C., 'The Kamehameha Early Education Program' in Jordan, C. et al., *A Multidisciplinary Approach to Research in Education*, Technical Report 81, Kamehameha Schools, Bernice, P., Bishop Estate, Honolulu, 1977.
55. Katz, M., 'Pre-School Children on an Outer Island in Fiji'. Unpublished paper, Institute of Pacific Studies, University of the South Pacific, Suva, Fiji, 1978.
56. Keesing, F.M., *Education in Pacific Countries*, Kelly and Walsh, Shanghai, 1937.
57. Keesing, F. & M., *Elite Communication in Samoa*, Stanford University Press, Stanford, 1956.
58. Kennell, J.H. & Klaus, M.H., *Maternal–Infant Bonding*, Mosby, St. Louis, 1976.
59. King, M., *Te Puea*, Hodder and Stoughton, Wellington, 1977.
60. Lawrence, P., 'Looking Beyond Ourselves: Aspects of Early Childhood Care in Other Countries' in O'Rourke, B., and Clough, J. (eds), *Early Childhood in New Zealand*, Heinemann Educational Books, Auckland, 1978.
61. Levy, R.I., *Tahitians*, University of Chicago Press, Chicago, 1973.
62. Lewin, R., 'Starved Brains', *Psychology Today*, 29–33, September, 1975.
63. Lewis, O., *Life in a Mexican Village*, University of Illinois, Urbana, 1951.

64. Linton, A. and Wagley, C., *Ralph Linton*, Columbia University Press, New York, 1971.
65. McArthur, N., *Island Populations of the Pacific*, Australian National University, Canberra, 1968.
66. McClelland, D.C., *The Achieving Society*, Van Nostrand, New Jersey, 1961.
67. MacDonald, G., 'Pre-School and Parent Education for Minorities' in *Equality of Opportunity in Education*, Association for the Study of Childhood, Wellington, 1972.
68. MacDonald, G., *Maori Mothers and Pre-School Education*, Whitcombe & Tombs, Christchurch, 1973.
69. MacDonald, S. and Gallimore, R., *Battle in the Classroom*, Intext, Scranton, 1971.
70. MacKenzie, M., 'Who is a Good Mother?', *Ethnomedicine*, Vol. 4, No. 1/2, 7–22, 1976/77.
71. Malo, T., 'Rotuman Marriage' in Plant, C. (ed.). *Rotuma: Split Island*, Institute of Pacific Studies, University of the South Pacific, Suva, 1977.
72. Manihera Te Uira, 'Postscript' in Ritchie, Jane, *Chance To Be Equal*, Cape Catley, Picton, 1978.
73. Marshall, D., *Island of Passion Ra'ivavae*, George Allen & Unwin, London, 1962.
74. Mason, L., *The Many Faces of Micronesia*, Vol. 1, No. 1 of Pacific Asian Studies, January 1975.
75. Mead, Margaret, *Coming of Age in Samoa*, William Morrow, New York, 1928. (Our quotations and pagination are from the Pelican edition, 1943.)
76. Mead, M., 'Homogeneity and Hypertrophy: A Polynesian Based Hypothesis' in Highland, G.A., Force, R.W., Howard, A., Kelly, K., Sinoto, Y.H., (eds), *Polynesian Culture History*, Bishop Museum Press, Honolulu, 1967.
77. Metge, J., *The Maoris of New Zealand*, Routledge Kegan Paul, London, 1976.
78. Minturn, L., and Lambert, W.L., *Mothers of Six Cultures*, Wiley, New York, 1964.
79. Mischel, W., *Personality and Assessment*, Wiley, New York, 1968.
80. Mishkin, B., 'The Maori of New Zealand' in Mead, M. (ed.), *Cooperation and Competition Among Primitive Peoples*, McGraw-Hill, New York, 1937.
81. Morgan, P., *Child Care, Sense and Fable*, Temple Smith, London, 1975.
82. Munroe, R.L. & Munroe, R.H., *Cross-Cultural Human Development*, Brooks-Cole, California, 1975.
83. Nurcombe, B., *Children of the Dispossessed*, University Press of Hawaii, Honolulu, 1976.
84. Oliver, D., *My Friends The Shoeshine Boys*, YMCA, Suva, 1977.
85. Oliver, D., *Ancient Tahitian Society*, University Press of Hawaii, Honolulu, 1974.

86. Ord, I.G., *Mental Tests for Préliterates*, Jacaranda, Brisbane, 1971.
87. *Pacific Islands Yearbook*, Pacific Publications, Sydney, 1978.
88. Parkinson, S.V., 'Some Observations on the Cause of Malnutrition in Pacific Urban Communities' in Harre, J. (ed.), *Living in Town*, South Pacific Social Science Association, Suva, 1973.
89. Pitt, D., and MacPherson, C., *Emerging Pluralism: Samoan Community in New Zealand*, Longman Paul, Auckland, 1974.
90. Redfield, R., *The Little Community*, Chicago University Press, Chicago, 1955.
91. Ritchie, James, *The Making of a Maori*, A.H. & A.W. Reed, Wellington, 1963.
92. Ritchie, James, 'The Making of a Maori' in Howard, A. (ed.), *Polynesia: Readings on a Culture Area*, Chandler Publishing Company, USA, 1971.
93. Ritchie, James, 'Teaching the Social Sciences: Innovation in small systems', *Topics in Culture Learning*, Vol. 1, No. 1, East West Center, Hawaii, 1973.
94. Ritchie, Jane, *Childhood in Rakau*, Victoria University, Wellington, 1957.
95. Ritchie, Jane, *Tamariki Maori*, Centre for Maori Studies and Research, University of Waikato, 1977.
96. Ritchie, Jane, *Chance To Be Equal*, Cape Catley, Picton, 1978.
97. Ritchie, Jane and James, *Child Rearing Patterns in New Zealand*, A.H. & A.W. Reed, Wellington, 1970.
98. Ritchie, Jane and James, *Growing Up in New Zealand*, George Allen & Unwin, Sydney, 1978.
99. Ritchie, Jane and James, 'Child Rearing and Child Abuse: The Polynesian Context' in Jill Korbin (ed.), *Child Abuse: a Cross-Cultural Perspective*, Garland, N.Y. (in press).
100. Ritchie, Jane and James, 'Children of Poverty' in Stewart, R.A.C. (ed.), *Child Development in New Zealand* (in press).
101. Rohner, R.P., *They Love Me, Love Me Not*, HRAF Press, New Haven, 1975.
102. Rutter, M., *Maternal Deprivation Reassessed*, Penguin, Harmondsworth, 1972.
103. Salmond, Ann, *Hui*, A.H. & A.W. Reed, Wellington, 1975.
104. Schoeffel, P., 'The Origins and Development of Womens' Associations in Western Samoa: 1830–1977', *Journal of Pacific Studies*, in press, 1978.
105. Seeto, M., *Pre-School Education in Fiji: A Survey*, Master's Thesis in Education, University of Auckland, 1976.
106. Silva, P., *One Thousand Dunedin Three Year Olds*, Report to the Medical Research Council, Dunedin, 1976.
107. Sloggett, B.B., 'Use of Group Activities and Team Rewards to Increase Individual Classroom Productivity', *Teaching Exceptional Children*, 54–66, Winter, 1971.

108. Sloggett, B.B., Gallimore, R. & Kubany, E., 'A Comparative Analysis of Fantasy, Need Achievement Among High and Low Achieving Male Hawaiian–Americans, *Journal of Cross Cultural Psychology*, Vol. 1, No. 1, 53–61, 1970.
109. Thomas, D.R., 'Cooperation and Competition among Polynesian and European Children', *Child Development*, Vol. 46, No. 1, 984–953, 1975.
110. Thomas, D.R., 'Cooperation and Competition among Children in the Pacific Islands and New Zealand: The School as an Agent of Social Change', *Journal of Research and Development in Education*, 1978, in press.
111. Thompson, L., *Southern Lau*, Bernice P. Bishop Museum, Bulletin No. 162, Honolulu, 1940.
112. Tonkin, S., 'Post-Neonatal Infant Deaths in the Auckland Hospital Board Area, 1972', *New Zealand Medical Journal*, Vol. 81, No. 534, 187–190, 1975.
113. Vayda, A.P. & Rappaport, R.A., 'Island Cultures' in Harding, T.G. and Wallace, B.J., *Cultures of the Pacific*, Free Press, New York, 1970.
114. Waqa, M., *The Youth of Fiji*, Institute of Pacific Studies, University of the South Pacific, Suva, 1977.
115. Wendt, A., *Pouliuli*, Longman Paul, Auckland, 1977.
116. Werner, E.G., Bierman, J.M. and French, F.E., *The Children of Kauai*, University of Hawaii Press, Honolulu, 1971.
117. Weisner, T.S. & Gallimore, R., 'My Brother's Keeper: Child and Sibling Caretaking', *Current Anthropology*, Vol. 18, No. 2, 169–190, 1977.
118. Yen, D.E. & Gordon, J. (eds), *Anuta: A Polynesian Outlier in the Solomon Islands*, Pacific Anthropological Records, No. 21, Bishop Museum Press, Honolulu, 1973.

Index

Abortion, 16, 39, 40, 41
Abuse, child, 157, 158
Achievement, 72–79,
 and school, 121, 128, 132
 and status, 81
Adolescence, 24
 ceremonies at, 88, 89
 contrast with West, 89
 and education, 93
 fertility in, 40
 identity in, 93
 language in, 111
 peer groups and, 61, 91
 Polynesian concept of, 94
 suicide, 139
Adoption, 27, 33–36, 62, 40, 42
Adorno, T.W., 163
Adultery, 96
Affiliation, 73
Affluence, primitive, 101
Aggression, 102, 138, 157
Aiga (extended family), 21, 28, 138
Aitutaki, 88
Alcohol, 100, 137, 138, 159
Ali'i, (aristocrat), 82, 98
Alor, 51
Anuta, 50
Anxiety, coping with, 95
 sexual, 100–101
Aoyagi, M., 45, 163
Ari'i, (chief), 82
Ariki, (chief),
 (see also Aliki, 82, Ari'i, 98)
Atea, (sky), 25
Atolls, 16, 18, 19
Attachment,
 maternal, 38, 154–155

Au'uluma, (unmarried women's association), 91, 98
Auckland, 18
Aumaga (association of utitled men), 91
Ausubel, D., 73, 163
Authoritarianism, 86
Avoidance, kinship, 32

Barnett, H.G., 163
Beaglehole, E., 92, 152, 163
Beaglehole, E. & P., 10, 11, 40, 50, 62, 90, 163
Beeby, C., 110, 127, 163
Behaviour modification, 132
Benedict, R., 80, 149, 163
Bernard, J., 163
Bierman, J.M., 168
Best, E., 163
Biggs, B., 163
Bilingualism, 140, 141
Bobillier, C., 126, 163
Bonding, 38, 76, 154
Books, 112, 113, 115, 116
Bowlby, J., 163
Breast feeding, 45, 160
Bronfenbrenner, V., 147, 163
Bure, (house), 38
Burrows, E.G., 29, 164

Caretaking
 sibling, 18, 63–66, 76–77
 education, 71, 143
Carroll, V., 164
Ceremonies, 22, 92, 93
 at adolescence, 88
 children's participation in, 85

Growing up in Polynesia

kava, 82
learning of, 107
Chandra, S., 164
Chiefs
 authority of, 17
 (see also *Matai, Ariki*)
Child care, collective, 20, 27
 and women's role, 103
Christianity, influence of, 22, 72, 123
 (see also Missionaries)
Church, 22, 139, 144, 160
Circumcision, 90
 (see also supercision)
Clay, M., 164
Climate, effects of, 16
Clubs, at adolescence, 61
Cole, M., 154, 164
Community, 20–26, 79
 alienation from, 25
 changes in, 15
 and child abuse, 159
 dependency on, 58
 obligations, 80
 and preschool, 115, 119
 and school, 121–135
Competition, 72, 78, 80, 128–129
 (see also cooperation)
Conflicts, 23, 25, 96, 123, 150–152, 157
Contraception, 42, 105
Control, parental, 70
Cook Islands,
 malnutrition, 46
 population of, 137
 rituals at adolescence, 89–90
 children, 128
Cooperation, 70, 78, 80, 128–129
Crafts, 18, 122, 158
Creche, 37, 120
Crime, 101, 133, 157
Crocombe, R., 164
Curriculum, in preschools, 113

Danielsson, B., 41, 49, 56, 62, 164
Death, 19
Dependency, inhibition of, 59
De Vos, G.A., 164
Diet, changes in, 17

Discipline, 49, 146
Disease, 19
Drop-outs, 126, 132, 157–158
Dubois, C., 164

Earle, M., 68, 164
Economy,
 changes in, 19
 children's role in, 60
 and education, 107
 women's role in, 43, 57, 96
Education, 17, 106–120, 121–135
 and adolescence, 193
 dame school, 110, 127
 and disadvantage, 110
 early childhood, 106–120
 language of, 140
 multi-racial, 145
 primary, 106, 115
 secondary, 106–107
 and sibling caretakers, 71
 and status, 80, 86
 tertiary, 106–107, 126
 traditional, 107
Entertainment,
 changes in, 17
 children's, 67–68
Environment, 15–19
 dangers in, 17–18, 56, 143
Erikson, E., 147, 164
examinations, 121, 125–127

Fa'a fa fine, (transvestite male), 100
Fa'a Samoa, (Samoan way of life), 117, 137
Fakaleiti, (transvestite male), 100
Fale, (house), 21, 24
Family, extended, 20
Family,
 nuclear, 28, 30, 36, 109
 relationships, 17–18
 size, 19, 40
 western, 30–31, 37, 77, 109
Fanau, (children), 28
Fergusson, D.M., 164
Fertility, 19, 27, 40
Feti'i, 28

Fiji, 8
  birth practices, 39, 43–44
  boys, 70
  and chiefs, 82
  contraception, 42
  naming in, 45
  preschool in, 118
  supercision in, 90
Firth, R., 10, 41, 164
Fono, (village meeting), 95
Fonua, (placenta), 44
Fostering, 35, 62
Frankovitch, M.K., 164
French, F.E., 168
Frisbee, R., 107, 164
Fua'i fale, (household), 21
Futuna, kin avoidance in, 32

Gadd, B., 164
Gallimore, R., 11, 32, 52, 57–58, 62, 64, 73, 75, 86, 110, 126, 164, 166, 168
Gangs, 91
Geddes, W.R., 39, 164
Genealogy, 29, 35, 40, 81
Gerrand, N., 116, 164
Ghosts, 49, 55
Gladwin, T., 164
Gods, 18
Goldman, I., 80, 164
Gordon, J., 168
Graves, N.B., and T.D., 67–68, 128, 165
Griffen, V., 165

Haka, (male dance), 145
Hangi, (earth oven), 97
Hapu, (tribe), 30
Hardy, M., 165
Hau'ofa, E., 42, 105, 165
Hawaii, 18
  abortion in, 41
  achievement motivation in, 74–75
  adolescence groups, 91
  chiefs in, 82
  children's jobs, 67
  early indulgence in, 46
  independence training in, 58–59
  sex roles, 98
  sibling care taking, 62
Head Start, 110
Health,
  care, 161
  child, 19, 160
  mental, 151, 155
  services, 143, 161
  women's, 99, 105
Herangi, Te Puea, 124
Heuer, B., 40, 165
Hine, (female child), 31, 81
Holmes, L.D., 45–46, 55, 62, 67, 90, 97, 101, 165
Horner, M., 78, 165
Howard, A., 11, 46, 58, 62, 75–77, 111, 165
Howarth, A.T.S., 165
Hui, (gathering), 92, 101
Hula, (dance), 145

Identity, 79, 93, 134, 162
Ihimaera, W., 134
Incest, 33
independence, training in, 52–59
Indulgence, early, 39, 46, 49–54
Infanticide, 16, 39, 40–42, 96
Isa, (longing), 90
Islands, high, 18
Iwi, (tribe, bone), 30

Jordan, C., 52, 165

Kai rangatira, (chiefly food), 97
Kainga, (family), 28
Katz, M., 165
Kaumatua, (elder spokesman), 81, 101
Kava, (ceremonial drink), 82–83, 85, 91–92, 101, 122
Keesing, F. & M., 165
Kennel, J.H., 165
King, M., 195
Kingitanga, (King Movement), 98
Kinship, 21, 28, 37, 40
  classificatory, 29
  and status, 81
  terminology, 29–30

Kluckhohn, Florence, 9
Kore, (night), 25
Koro, (old man), 81
Kuia, (older woman), 81
Kwakiutl, 80

Lambert, W.L., 166
Language,
 bilingualism, 140
 complexity of, 155
 development of, 111, 155
 and migration, 139, 141–142
 Polynesian, 25, 112
 and school, 112, 140
 status, 130
Lau group, 40
 abortion in, 41
 birth in, 44
Lavalava, (cloth wrap), 24, 90
Lawrence, P., 165
Levy, R., 11, 40–41, 56–57, 62, 75, 88, 90, 102, 165
Lewin, R., 165
Lewis, O., 149, 165
Life expectancy, 99
Linton, R., 10, 166
Literacy, 113, 115, 122–124

McArthur, N., 50, 166
McClelland, D.C., 73–74, 166
McDonald, S., 132
MacDonald, G., 166
MacKenzie, M., 46, 166
MacPherson, C., 138, 167
Mahu, (transvestite male), 100
Male roles, 95–105,
 and achievement, 76
 and boys, 64
 economic, 97
 and education, 122
 and initiation, 88
 and status, 96, 100–101, 150
 status language and, 111
Malnutrition, 46, 160
Malo, T., 40, 92, 166
Mana, (prestige), 22, 81–82, 121,
 and literacy, 123
Manihera, Te U., 124, 166

Maori, adolescence groups in, 91
 and abortion, 40–41
 achievement motivation, 73
 adoption, 36
 attitudes to preschool education, 108
 and birth, 43
 child rearing, 143
 community, 23
 education, 107
 identity at adolescence, 89
 infant mortality, 50
 kinship terms, 31, 81
 language, 29, 140
 naming, 45
 nutrition, 46
 preschool project, 115–117
 sex roles, 98, 101
 sibling caretaking, 62
 status, 83
Marae, (ceremonial meeting ground), 81, 83, 99, 101
marriage, 17, 99–100
Marshall, D., 40, 166
Mason, L., 17, 166
Matai, 91, 147
 authority of, 15, 17
 role of, 101, 104
 status of, 82–83, 94
Matua, (parent), 31–32
Matuatane, (father), 29
Mead, M., 10–11, 26, 28, 32, 40, 57, 62, 67, 71, 76, 83, 98, 111, 147, 157
Melanesia, 8
 and breast feeding, 45
 and status, 82
Menstruation, 40–41, 90, 96
Metge, M., 30, 81, 90, 166
Micronesia, 17
Migration, 16, 42, 136–145
 frustrations of, 139
 preparation for, 133–134, 142
Minturn, L., 166
Mischel, W., 166
Missionaries, 148
 and education, 110
 and infanticide, 41

and dress, 24
and literacy, 122–123
Moana-nui-a-Kiwa, (Maori: Pacific Ocean), 9
Modeling, 76
Mokopuna, (grandchild), 31, 34, 81
Morgan, P., 166
Mortality, infant, 49
Montessori, 100
Motivation, achievement, 72–74
Munroe, R.L. & R.H., 166
Mythology, 16, 25, 29

Naming, 44–45, 89, 103
Niue,
 rituals at adolescence, 89
 preschools in, 119
 population of, 137
Nopeli, (nobles), 82
Nurcombe, B., 166
Nutrition, 46, 50, 160
Nu'u, (village), 21

Oliver, Dennis, 70, 166
Oliver, Douglas, 41, 166
Oratory, 22, 112, 130
 Maori, 30, 81
 and status, 82
Ord, I.G., 167

Palau, 44, 50, 131
Papa-tu-a-nuku, (earth; earth mother) (also *Papa*), 16, 25, 29
Papua New Guinea,
 breast feeding, 45
 and education, 125, 128, 131
 and status, 82
Parenting,
 multiple, 28, 37–38, 65, 154
 solo, 35
Parent-teacher associations, 131
Pareu, (cloth wrap), 104
Parkinson, S.V., 167
Peers, 17, 60–71
 and achievement motivation, 75
 and language, 155
 and status, 84–85

Penrhyn, 89–90
Piaget, J., 147
Pitcairn, 26
Pito, (umbilical cord), 39, 44
Pitt, D., 138, 167
Plant, C., 166
Play centre, 116–117, 119
Poi, (female dance), 145
Politics,
 village, 23
 and women, 104
Polynesia, 7–9
 children's jobs in, 66–67
 cultures of, 16, 19
 defined, 7
 education, traditional, 107
 environment of, 15, 19
 family in, 18
 identify, 79
 kinship, 21, 28, 37
 languages of, 16, 112
 population control, 19
 resilience of, 145
 sibling caretaking in, 66
 status system, 80–87
Population, 105
 limitation of, 19, 42
Praise, 76, 118, 156
Pregnancy, 16, 42–43
Preschool, 106–120
 attitudes to, 108
 and community, 120
 curriculum, 113
 equipment, 117
 Fijian, 118
 freeplay, 108–109, 113, 115
 Head Start, 110
 models of, 108–110
 Montessori method, 109
 and structure, 114
 Te Kohanga, 114–116
 Tongan, 117–118
 Western Samoan, 117
Privacy, 22, 24
Pukapuka,
 abortion in, 40
 birth practices, 43–44
 and chiefs, 82

174 Growing up in Polynesia

family in, 28
initiation in, 99
kinship avoidance, 32
Pumehana, 52–53
Punishment, 49, 53, 55, 85, 114, 146, 156–157

Race,
  mixed, 35
Ra'ivavae, 19, 40
Rakau studies, 11, 73, 62, 68, 74
Rangatira, (aristocrat), 81
Rangi, (father), 25, 29
Rangiatea, (abode of skyfather), 25
Rappaport, R.A., 168
Raroia, 49, 56
  sibling caretaking, 62
  children's jobs in, 66
Reading, 112–113, 115
Redfield, R., 149, 167
Rejection, 50–54
  by community, 22
Respect, 32, 53–54, 86, 118, 129–130
Rewards, 77, 114, 118
Ritchie, James, 167
Ritchie, Jane, 167
Ritchie, Jane and James, 167
Rites de passage, 58
Rohner, R., 50, 167
Roles, sex, 37, 88, 95–105
  female
  male
  transvestite, 100
Rongo, (god of agriculture), 25
Rotuma, 11,
  achievement motivation in, 76, 77
  sexual freedom in, 40
  religion, 21
  sibling caretaking in, 62
Rutter, M., 167

Salmond, A., 167
Samoa,
  achievement in, 76
  acquisition of status, 92–93
  adult transition, 91
  agriculture, 101
  birth practices, 43–44
  breast feeding in, 45
  brother-sister avoidance, 32
  chiefs in, 82–83, 87
  children's' jobs in, 67
  community in, 21
  infant clothing, 46
  infant mortality, 50
  migration, 138
  naming in, 45
  politics, 23
  preschool education in, 117
  punishment in, 102
  sexual activities, 40
  sex roles in, 97–98
Schoeffel, P., 167
School, 121–135
  and child caretakers, 143
  and community, 121–135
  and disadvantage, 110
  dropouts, 126, 132, 157–158
  language of, 112, 140–141
  success in, 77, 111, 125–126
School Certificate, 125
Seeto, M., 167
Sex roles, 37, 88, 95–105
Sexual activity, 40, 92, 96, 102
  standards, 92
Sibling,
  caretaking, 62–64, 76–77
  rivalry, 48, 86
Silva, P., 167
Siva, (dance), 145
Sloggett, B., 132, 167–168
Socialisation,
  and community, 161
  and education, 111, 124–125
  goals of, 146–147
  intensity of, 77
  peer, 64–65, 70, 155
  and reading, 112
  urban, 144
Stages, of development, 58
Status, 23, 26, 80–87
  and achievement, 73
  adoption and, 35
  ceremonial, 92
  and early independence, 53
  and education, 80, 86

Index

kinship and, 33, 81
initiation, 88–94
nutrition and, 46
language of, 111, 130
and migration, 138, 143
sexual, 92
socioeconomic, 86
of teachers, 111
Tongan women, 97
of women, 95–105
Status rivalry, 26, 48, 53
Success,
  fear of, 78
  learning from, 114
Supercision, 88, 90

Tahiti,
  abortion in, 40–41
  and birth, 43
  chiefs in, 82
  children's work in, 67
  infanticide in, 41
  sex roles in, 102
  sexual activity, 40, 90
  sibling caretaking, 62
  supercision in, 88
  women in, 102
Tama, (father), 29
Tama, (male child), 31
Tamai, (father or child), 29
Tamure, (dance), 145
Tane, (man), 25
Tangaroa, (sea god), 25
Tangata waka wanau, (priestly male), 43
Tapa, (bark cloth), 18, 24, 43
Tapu, 99
Tattoo, 92
Ta'u, 12, 101
Taupou, (village maiden), 91
Tawhiao, King, 124
Teacher,
  and the community, 115
  and schools, 121–135
  status of, 111
Teina, (younger brother), 81
Te Kohanga, 114–116
Thomas, D.R., 78, 128, 168

Thompson, L., 40, 168
Tikopia,
  fertility control in, 40
  infanticide in, 41
Time Magazine, 17
Tohunga, (expert), 42, 81
Toilet training, 46
Tokelau, 137
  brother-sister avoidance, 32
Tonga,
  birth, 39, 43–44
  breast feeding, 45
  brother-sister avoidance, 32
  children's jobs, 67
  education in, 106–107
  infant mortality in, 50
  origins, 19
  preschool education in, 117–118
  politics, 23
  sex roles in, 88, 98
  status in, 82, 87
  status of women, 97
  supercision in, 90
Tongareva, 29
  brother-sister avoidance, 32
Tonkin, S., 168
Transvestite role, 100
Tribe, 30
Truancy, 126, 132
Tu, (god of war), 25
Tuahine, (sister), 81
Tuakana, (older brother), 81
Tungane, (brother), 81
Tupuna, (ancestor), 31–32, 81
Turangawaewae, (place to stand), 21

Uma, (earth oven), 43, 97
Urban,
  environment, 139, 143, 157
  education, 144
  and childrearing, 144, 159
  community development, 134
  and diet, 160
  and work, 141–142
Uvaea,
  brother-sister avoidance, 32

Values, cultural, 23, 58, 148
Vayda, A.P., 168

Wahine, (woman), 81
Waikato, land wars in, 124
Wakawawine, (transvestite male), 100
Wanau, (family), 28
Waqa, M., 125, 168
Warfare, 16, 19
Weisner, T.S., 64, 86, 168
Wendt, A., 94, 134, 168
Werner, E.G., 168
Whaea, (mother), 29
Whakaiti, (obligation to be humble), 82
Whamere, (family), 30
Whanau, (extended family), 28, 30, 46–47, 130
Whare Wananga, (School of learning), 122
Whenua, (land; placenta), 16–17, 44
Whiting, J. & B., 154

Women, 150
 and birth, 43
 clothing of, 24
 and education, 107
 economic role, 43, 57, 96–97, 103
 and fear of success, 78–79
 and fertility control, 41–42
 girls roles, 65
 and health, 99
 liberation of, 105
 roles, 95–105
 status of, 23, 36, 41, 96, 98, 104
Work
 and children, 122, 132, 133
 and migration, 136, 141–142
 and subsistence, 101–102
 and women, 97, 103, 154

Yen, D.E., 168